Frank Jamieson Ryan

Protestant miracles. High orthodox and evangelical authority for the belief in divine interposition in human affairs

Compiled from the writings of men eminent in Protestant churches

Frank Jamieson Ryan

Protestant miracles. High orthodox and evangelical authority for the belief in divine interposition in human affairs
Compiled from the writings of men eminent in Protestant churches

ISBN/EAN: 9783337157326

Printed in Europe, USA, Canada, Australia, Japan

Cover: Foto ©Lupo / pixelio.de

More available books at **www.hansebooks.com**

Protestant Miracles.

HIGH ORTHODOX AND EVANGELICAL AUTHORITY FOR
THE BELIEF IN DIVINE INTERPOSITION
IN HUMAN AFFAIRS.

SOME ACCOUNT OF MARVELOUS CURES OF ILLNESS,
RESCUE FROM DANGER, DEATH, POVERTY AND
SUFFERING, THROUGH FAITH AND PRAYER,
IN RECENT CENTURIES.

Compiled from the Writings of Men Eminent in Protestant Churches.

By F. J. Ryan.

Stockton, Cal.
Record Publishing Co., Printers.
1899.

PREFACE.

This work was begun with very little thought that it would ever become a book. Its origin is this: I had been reading and hearing lectures on Christian Science, on metaphysical healing; mental science, etc., for some months, when there seemed to be almost a general onslaught on the first named system of religion and therapeutics, by orthodox clergymen, newspaper writers, coroners and other public officers, even to legislators. The animosity appeared to reach its climax in my home city just about the time the Scientist congregation announced as the subject of its Wednesday evening meeting, "Is Christian Science a Delusion?"

In examining the affirmative side of the proposition I found the basis thereof to be a Protestant dogma to the effect that the age of miracles had passed away with the immediate successors to the apostles. I also found that the men who held to this dogma prayed with apparent fervor for especial blessings upon their favorite charities, Sabbath schools, enterprises, and about the time the onslaught was made, that orthodox Protestant clergymen were lobbying for appointment as chaplains to several legislative bodies where they must pray for the rare miracles of the investment of those bodies with wisdom.

I remembered well the stories told by revivalists in my youth—I hadn't heard any revival sermons for a generation—of how they were aided in their work by miraculous means.

I remembered also that some clergymen had regarded the assassins, Booth and Guiteau, as instruments of Providence. It didn't matter that these were ministers of the gospel of hatred when their sectional prejudices were stirred. I never heard of any of them being disciplined for what Northern clergymen of the same churches usually regarded as blasphemy. With these matters in mind I set about investigating the truth or falsity of the plea that Protestants agreed on the proposition that the age of miracles had passed away with the second century of our era. I was astounded at the result of my first week's search by finding that many of the most responsible, scholarly, eminent and effective laborers in the Protestant field of Christianity, in every century, and perhaps in every year since the Reformation, including Luther, have not only believed in but put themselves on record as believing in miraculous healing of the sick; of the rescue of the righteous from death by storm, by flood, by fire, by accident, by crime, by freezing and other means, in answer to prayer. I have also found cases in which clergymen have endorsed, as true, stories of the vindication of just persons from grave accusations of crime and other miraculous occurrences; of special providences and divine interpositions in human affairs for the promotion of religion and justice.

In pursuing my researches for material I have examined several hundred volumes by authors of acknowledged ability, learning and authority. While I have found something of value in nearly every work, many of them contain matter that is in substance repetitions of some other authors. Some are amusing for the simplicity they seem to ascribe to their readers. This class, though it includes some of the most learned and famous, seems to suppose the reader will not or cannot detect discrepancies of statement or inconsistences of argument, when the inconsistent or incompatible statements or arguments are widely separated.

Some are intrinsically and apparently intentionally amusing. Of this class is Scientific Sophisms," by Samuel Wainwright, D. D. While it does not defend miracles it ridicules that class of scientists who seem to require readers to reject the supernatural for the hyper-natural, who spin metaphysical theories as intangible and unintelligible and that convey as little information on the subject to the average mind as do the clouds that chase each other or tumble and roll over each other during a summer storm. These theorists seem to expect their reader to play Polinius to their Hamlet and declare that they see in those nebulous theories whales, camels or weasels, as the theorist may suggest, without detecting the inconsistency or absurdity of the theories or assumptions.

In reading the various hypotheses advanced by materialists—philosophers real and presumptive—to explain away miracles, the conclusion is often forced on the reader that it requires more credulity to accept the theory than to accept the miracle. They seem to imagine that in calling marvelous occurrences "phenomena" they have disposed of the question. It never seems to occur to them that their writings will be read by those who can distinguish between matters of terminology and matters of logic, or that any will perceive that to call a miracle a phenomenon does not take it out of the realm of the miraculous.

It may strike some of those who read this work that the authorities I quote in support of the opinion that the age of miracles has not passed away, do not agree well. That must be granted, but the disagreement is principally as to what are miracles. However inconsistent the arguments of one may be with those advanced by others, the inconsistency is no concern of mine. The main fact remains that most of those from whom I quote deserve to rank as leaders of Protestant thought and others are, at least, non-Catholic, so that in quoting them I am consistent with the purpose I had in view in undertaking to show that Protestants, under which classification I include all who are neither Catholics, Jews, Atheists, Spiritualists, Swedenborgians nor anti-Christians, are by no means unanimous in the belief that no real miracles have been wrought since the death of the immediate successors of the apostles.

Some may want to know who is the author of this little volume. He is a very obscure person and his personality is not involved. If the reader doubts anything stated herein as fact, he doubts not the author but the authority to whom he refers or whom he quotes. He has sought to verify his statements and, as far as possible, has confined himself to works that may be found in almost all public libraries in cities of say half a century's growth. The author is old in newspaper work, but this department of literary work is new to him and critics will probably see in it the evidence of journalistic journey-work and lack of literary finish—the ornamentals of book-architecture. These were not the object of the work and I have made fact the first object and argument the second. If the few arguments are good and well based they need neither a celebrated name nor the gilding, molding, carving or fillagree work of the word-artist to support them. On its merits this little book is respectfully submitted. F. J. R.

PROTESTANT DISBELIEF.

IT OVERSHOT ITS MARK AND CAUSED ITS AUTHORS TROUBLE.

When it is asserted, as it often is, that the age of miracles has long been passed, it becomes a matter of interest to know when the age ended. The time usually given, by those who regard themselves as orthodox Christians, is the end of the second century. They rarely go into particulars as to the exact year or even the decade, but the impression gained is that miracles went out about the time that Constantine made Christianity fashionable.

Constantine embraced Christianity A. D. 313 and his conversion was one of the last miracles that are now generally recognized as genuine by orthodox Protestants. Catholics believe that miracles are still wrought by men of exceptionally pure and Christ-like lives. Even Father DeSmet, in his letters from the missions, in what was then Oregon territory, tells of some phenomena that were miraculous and, if my memory is not at fault, among them were the exorcising of evil spirits. I cannot now find the letters to which I refer, but my recollection is that these stories were published in a Catholic weekly paper in St. Louis during about the years 1844 to 1848. It will not do to quote Catholic authority, however, as Protestants generally discredit their accounts. Even the authors of the Bampton lectures, whose object is to defend the Gospel accounts of miracles against disbelievers, discredit Catholic miracles and ignore all other miracles than those recorded in the canonical scriptures. The same course of reasoning adopted by the Bampton lectures would suffice to substantiate other accounts of miracles, but the lectures skillfully avoid that conclusion by ignoring the events presented as miraculous.

For the purpose of the argument the word "miracle" is here employed in the ordinary sense in which it is popularly employed, viz: An event occurring or effect brought about by means beyond or above the natural laws known to physical science.

As a rule orthodox Protestants scout all accounts of modern miracles, but there are exceptions to the rule; notably among the revivalists who in their zeal tell the most marvelous stories of divine preservation of life; rescue from death by accident, famine, pestilence or assassination.

THE BAMPTON LECTURES.

EFFORTS OF PROTESTANTS TO ARREST THE RESULT OF THEIR OWN DOUBTS.

The efforts of Protestants to discredit and cause disbelief in "Catholic" miracles had an unforeseen effect. It aroused a spirit of investigation and one effect of that was the gradual discrediting not only of all ecclesiastical and apostolic miracles but widespread attacks on the belief in miracles of any kind. This skepticism seems to have invaded the churches and the inroads of the spirit of inquiry, skepticism and criticism were so great that the churches found themselves compelled to take the defensive.

In the course of time the ablest men in all the orthodox churches were retained to deliver sermons and lectures; to write replies to and refutations of the arguments of those who discredited or belittled miracles in any age. The result is a vast mass of literature, widely diffused; much of it conflicting and inconsistent, but all tending to preserve the foundation of orthodoxy, which, if miracles and myths should be proved to be synonymous, would crumble like the mortar in the Budensiek tenement house of New York (which was made principally of mud) and bury many pious people in the ruins.

The Bampton lecture series was one of the most notable of the organized defenses of the miraculous origin of Chris-

PROTESTANT MIRACLES.

tianity. The fund to support these lectures was a bequest by John Bampton, canon of Salisbury, who died in 1751 and left his wealth in trust to support the lecture courses.

John Tyndall deals without mercy with the distinction between miracles and special providences which Dr. Mozley, one of the Bampton lecturers, attempted to establish. In "Fragments of Science," page 379, Tyndall says arguments against modern miracles are quite as forcible against ancient, in which all Christians believe, and adds that in the "fascination of a desire to establish or avoid a certain result—a favorite pastime with some minds—they mix proof and trust, which was dangerous to scientific minds. What must it be to Mozley's indiscriminate audiences."

Lecky, in his "Rationalism in Europe," shows how men, whose minds had once been started in the direction of doubt of the miraculous, rushed from polytheism past monotheism to atheism and placed the clergy and the churchmen in general in the awkward position of teaching the miraculous of the past and denying the possibility of it in the present. The inconsistency of orthodoxy, so far as the established church of England is concerned, is illustrated by a controversy "Christianity and Agnosticism," published by Appleton & Co. in 1889. In that volume three eminent English churchmen, Henry Wace, D. D., the Bishop of Peterboro, and W. H. Mallock, combined their talents in an effort to refute the arguments of Prof. Thomas H. Huxley. A perusal of the volume will show how churchmen stagger under the burden they have assumed.

William Howitt, in speaking of the apostolic miracles, and

what appeared to be general Protestant disbelief in them, said: "If they are not true, Christianity is not true. If they are true, the fault lies with us if we lack the power of performing them; we have not the vital Christianity and only half Christianity." Howitt was a clergyman and was eminent in literature in his day.

EMINENT BELIEVERS IN MIRACLES.

It seems strange, passing strange, that those who have written volumes in defense of the gospel accounts of miracles should either ignore the accounts of apostolic miracles, those of the early fathers, or of latter years, yet this is done. E. A. Bertram, in his "Homeletic Encyclopaedia," quotes extensively from ecclesiastical writers from the earliest days in defense and explanation of the miracles of the gospels and follows these with equally extensive quotations from like writers to discredit later miracles. St. Augustine is first quoted to the effect that miracles had ceased and that they "would not move if not wonderful and if usual would not be wonderful." In a foot note, however, the compiler quotes later words of Augustine which say miracles were being wrought "even now," which was in the fifth century, Augustine's latest writings having been done in 429. All the other authorities quoted range from the eleventh century down to Henry Ward Beecher, except Gregory, who was so much of a wonder-worker that he was on that account surnamed Thaumaturgis. The accounts of the miracles he performed challenge the capacity of the reader to believe. Gregory died in the year 234, so that his testimony, as well as his miracles, may be left out of consideration.

PROTESTANT MIRACLES.

The late Cardinal Newman published a work on the miracles of the Roman Catholic church, but Protestants, of course, ignore it. It may be remarked, apropos of what is recognized or ignored by Protestants and sectarists (if they are not the same), that for years they ignored Newman's magnificent hymn, "Lead, Kindly Light," because, after he wrote it, he became a Catholic and a priest. It is the purpose here, however, to deal with Protestant doubt and effort to discredit all miracles of modern times, and especially the healing of diseases, so that Newman may be left out of the account for the present, at least.

EPISCOPAL MIRACLES.

WHY THEY AND BELIEF IN THEM ARE HARD TO FIND.
SOME STRIKING EXCEPTIONS TO THE RULE.

The reason this article, devoted to miracles and the belief in them in the Anglican church (which includes the Protestant-Episcopal church in the United States), is short, is that belief in modern miracles is discouraged by that organization. While the book of common prayer indicates a belief that God will comply with requests for blessings, the writers of the church have left very little record of events of a marvelous character or of a practical belief in the miraculous beyond the miracles of the bible.

A search of the available books on the subject resulted in the discovery of some striking exceptions to the rule of disbelief. Macaulay, in Vol. 1, page 61, of his history of England, says that it was objected to Henry VIII being the head of the church, that St. Paul had spoken of certain persons whom the Holy Ghost had made overseers and shepherds of the faithful. Henry's friends were ready with the answer that he was the very overseer, the very shepherd whom the Holy Ghost had appointed and to whom the expression of St. Paul applied. Among those who held that view was Cranmer, who taught that the royal and sacerdotal characters had been inseparably joined by divine ordinance.

When Elizabeth came to the throne this idea had to be remodeled and the thirty-seventh article of religion was accordingly framed. It declares that the ministering of God's word does not belong to princes, though Cranmer had previously declared that God had committed to Christian princes the whole care of all their subjects, as well concerning the administration of God's word for the cure of souls as concerning the administration of things political. In a foot note to page 62 Macaulay says "these are Cranmer's own words."

This exception to the rule of disbelief in the miraculous, was a political necessity, just as was its modification. It very naturally recalls what was said of Abraham Lincoln's opinion about hell. When asked, after hearing some stories of atrocities to Union soldiers in Confederate prisons, if he did not believe in hell, he is reported to have answered: "It may be a military necessity."

Protestantism in England in its early history was not favorable for the growth of miracles. It presented no encouragement of either climate or soil. So far was it from approving efforts at that part of the teachings of Jesus, that early in the eighteenth century it expelled certain of its ministers who believed in healing the sick, as will be seen elsewhere. It also caused the expulsion from England of certain French Protestant exiles who believed their leaders to be able to even raise the dead. A remnant of the sect thus expelled still exists in the United States, mostly in Pennsylvania, and its members are known as Schwenkfeldians. Other isolated remnants are occasionally met in other states and in Europe.

It did not extinguish all belief in miracle working, however. Conyers Middleton, D. D., who distinguished himself in the first half of the eighteenth century as a writer on religious and political subjects did not agree with the church of which he was a minister. In Leslie Stephen's "English Thought in the Eighteenth Century" Middleton is noticed quite extensively. Stephen says Middleton asked by insinuation if St. Augustine is discredited concerning miracles, why should Moses or Matthew be believed, and if Augustine is believed why not also accounts of modern miracles.

In recent years Canon Farrar, one of the most prominent prelates of the Church of England, takes both sides of the subject. In his "Lives of the Fathers" he speaks incredulously of the miracles ascribed to Gregory, who is classed as a saint by Catholics. He says Gregory had a weakness for collecting the bones of martyrs, but he also mentions, without question, miraculous cures attributed to those relics. He also tells of St. Augustine unconsciously healing Paulus and Palladia. The beneficiaries in this case were a young man and his sister, who, while seeking aid from the saint, fainted in his church. When they recovered consciousness, the infirmities of which they came to be healed had disappeared.

These are, of course, Catholic miracles but not "Popish," as they occurred at a time when there was no objection to popery. They are principally significant because they are mentioned by so high a church dignitary and authority as Canon Farrar, after his predecessors had so generally, and almost unanimously, treated Augustine as a deluder in the matter of his marvelous stories. Indeed, they quote him to the effect that no miracles were performed in his day, as if to prove him a liar on his own testimony.

The only miracle Farrar attributes directly to Augustine is quoted from the saint's biographer, Possidius. It is the healing of an unnamed sick man. On this Farrar comments:

> It must be classed with similar incidents and similar testimonies in all ages, even down to our own.

Further on he says such miracles stand on a level with the miracles wrought at the exhibitions of the Holy Coat of Treves, in Prussia. This Holy Coat is alleged to be that for which the Roman soldiers cast lots at the crucifixion, a mere sight of which cures all manner of ills, but it is a Catholic relic and the miracles are like unto it.

Butler (Catholic), in his "Lives of the Saints," quotes Dr. Cave, whom he describes as an eminent Protestant authority, in support of the miracles of St. Ambrose, as being well authenticated by evidence.

Among those clergymen of the English church who did not adopt the views of the majority on the subject was William Stephen Gilly, M. A., etc, prebendary of Durham. In a volume published in London in 1827 he quotes approvingly from Boyer's history of the Vaudois of the miraculous escape of those whom the Presbyterians claim as of their fold. The story is told elsewhere under the head of "Presbyterian Ideas."

If it were allowable to quote from books evidently published for Sunday school libraries, this chapter might be greatly enlarged, but I prefer to cite, with few exceptions, the cases that seem to be well authenticated by well known writers or clergymen of the church.

PRESBYTERIAN IDEAS.

LATTER DAY MIRACLES VIEWED WITH DISFAVOR BY CALVIN'S DISCIPLES.

Presbyterians furnish fewer evidences of a belief in the miraculous than most other sectarians. The spirit of the early Presbyterians which impelled rather than persuaded them to oppose everything that smacked of "popery" made them studiously avoid noticing events that seemed supernatural. Their records are not wholly destitute of such evidence, however

"Presbyterians" is the title of a work by Rev. George P. Hays, D. D. LL.D. It is a concise history of the origin and career of the churches of that denomination, with introductions by Rev. John Hall, D. D. LL.D., and Rev. William E. Moore, D. D. LL.D. Dr. Hays includes among Presbyterians the Waldenses of the continent of Europe, but he does not go so far as do thir own historians in ascribing their preservation to direct interposition of Providence. On page 40 of his work he says the Reformation and revival of religion were the results of the outpouring of the Spirit of God upon the church at large at a time when providences were fully ripe. On page 143 the historian, speaking of the "spiritual darkness" in which the eighteenth century closed, the loss of Harvard College to orthodox Congregationalists and the revival of A. D. 1800, says:

The problem of the time was to find some permanent system for reaching the whole country with the few available men on hand. God raised up choice men like Nettleton in Connecticut, Griffin in Boston, Finney in Ohio, etc. * * * * They were specially endowed with power from on high.

ORIGIN OF CAMP MEETINGS.

Dr. Hays tells how camp meetings originated with those Presbyterians who afterwards formed the Cumberland sect of that denomination, but he touches very lightly upon the "bodily exercises" of which Elders Jacob Knapp and Peter Cartwright said so much. He shows that it was the resort to revival methods that evolved the camp meeting, and what others call "the jerks" are very tamely described by him.

In a chapter written by two ministers of the Cumberland church, J. M. Howard and J. M. Hubbert, they say that when the proposition was made to Samuel McAdow for the revivalistic Presbyterians to secede and set up an independent synod, early in the nineteenth century, that pious man spent the whole night in prayer and in the morning announced that he had received sufficient light to justify him in joining the new movement. Thus the Cumberland Presbyterian church is in some measure, at least, dependent on an answer to man's prayers for its origin, although disbelief in the doctrines of predestination, and especially that part of it that taught infant damnation, was a powerful factor.

That this sect believe in direct communication of God to man, akin to inspiration, is evident in the way they defended the licensing to preach of men who had not been thoroughly

PRESBYTERIAN IDEAS.

educated. In the chapter devoted to the Cumberland church its authors say: "They believe that some who become religious late in life are called to preach the Gospel and that the strict Presbyterian rule would prevent these from obeying God's call."

Calvinism, as taught by the "regular" or original Presbyterians, deals with the miraculous in its origin. It teaches the doctrine of man's total depravity and that to be saved he must be born again. The miraculous feature of this teaching is found in the dogma that the new birth is not subject to man's will, but is the gift of the Holy Ghost. As the Holy Ghost is omnipotent and omniscient, He must have known from all eternity what He should do in all eternity to come. He must have known to whom He should give this new birth and herein is the dogma of election or predestination.

Another evidence of Presbyterian belief in divine interposition is given on page 93 of "Presbyterians," where the historian tells of the revivalists of 1740-41 entering churches to preach, against the objections of the pastors, on the ground that they had "the right to follow out what they called divine leading, even though nobody but themselves were able to understand the supposed providential indications."

The same historian quotes from a letter of Cotton Mather, of the year 1718, thus:

We are comforted with great numbers of the oppressed brethren coming from the north of Ireland. The glorious Providence of God in the removal hither of so many of a desirable class hath doubtless very great intentions in it.

Though Mather was not a Presbyterian, the people of whom he wrote were of that persuasion and the quotation of his words in the history may be regarded as a Presbyterian endorsement of special providences, alias miracles.

VAUDOIS MIRACLES.

A history of the Vaudois, or Waldenses, who are claimed as Presbyterians, by Antoine Monastier, one of their pastors, was translated by J. M. McClintock, who, in a preface to the American edition, wrote: "The Vaudois have been preserved from age to age amid the Alpine fastnesses and valleys of Piedmont—a perpetual testimony, at once to the providence of God and the persecuting cruelty of that ecclesiastical power which for centuries has 'exalted itself against God.'" Monastier, in describing a battle of the Vaudois against the papal troops sent to exterminate them in 1488, says the Vaudois prepared for the conflict by prayer. Their enemies, seeing them prostrate, ridiculed them, "being full of confidence in their own numbers, equipments and valor." The papist leader, LeNoir, is described as "another Goliath defying Israel, boasted with horrible blasphemies of the carnage he would make among the heretical herdsmen." Having incautiously raised his visor on account of the heat, a Vaudois arrow pierced his head and killed him. The historian thus attributes the result of the consequent flight of the papists: "But the Divine mercy secured the victory to the smaller number; God hearkened to those who relied on him."

Further along in the same chapter the historian describes the invaders trying to reach those of the Vaudois who had fled

PRESBYTERIAN IDEAS. 21

to an almost inaccessible spot, the Pra-di-torre. When they reached a narrow gorge they were suddenly enveloped in a fog so thick they dared not advance because they "could not distinguish a single object," and he continues:

The Angrognines, emboldened by this interposition of Providence in their favor, issued forth from their retreats, vigorously attacked their perplexed aggressors, whom they defeated, put to flight and pursued.

Monastier, on page 136 of his work, describes the Reformation as a miracle of mercy which "God was pleased to effect in many places," by raising up Luther, Zwingli and others as a result of the "direct intervention of Divine Providence." The work having been translated for the London Religious Tract Society, before the middle of the present century, naturally becomes an orthodox Protestant document by adoption, with all its belief in fifteenth century miracles.

As to the reality of Vaudois miracles, William Stephen Gilly, prebendary of Durham, who is referred to among Episcopal authorities, quotes approvingly from Boyer's history of that people of the miraculous escape of 800 or 900 of those Protestants from the country into which French and Sardinian oppression had driven them. Boyer says the country was guarded by 3000 hostile Catholic troops, which greatly increased the natural difficulties of the mountainous region. These Vaudois had been granted amnesty by the Duke of Sardinia, who also gave them liberty to settle in his dominions, and their victories over the hostile legions Boyer says formed a miraculous preservation of these Protestants from Catholic hostility. He further says of the change of heart of the Duke of Sardinia, that "God sent a spirit of division between the King of France and the Duke of Savoy, insomuch that they strove who should first gain the Vaudois to their party." (Boyer's Vaudois, page 226.)

This movement against the Vaudois began in 1686 and the divine interposition in their behalf was in 1690. This was nearly fourteen centuries after the time at which orthodox Protestants of to-day assert that the age of miracles ended.

A PRECOCIOUS PROPHET.

Rev. Dr. Alexander Carlyle tells in his autobiography how opposition to his appointment as minister at Inveresk, Scotland, was overcome. The position was in the gift of a certain nobleman who had promised it to him. The people wanted an older man, as Mr. Carlyle was not 24 when he was appointed, and were preparing to make his position uncomfortable.

The opponents were in the habit of frequenting a shop kept by a woman who had known Carlyle from infancy. When they spoke to her of an older man she told them they might as well be reconciled for Carlyle had been foreordained to the place—she heard him prophesy it when he was but 6 years old. The opponents were terrified at the idea of setting up opposition to a "meenister" sent by God, and especially one who had been foreordained to the place. The result was that he went there, won their love and remained fifty years.

This prophesy was simply an "auld wife's tale," but it illustrates the belief of the Scottish Presbyterian in the miraculous. Carlyle says the foundation for it was the old woman's fondness for him in his childhood. After caressing him as he stood on a stairhead at her shop, she expressed the hope that he should succeed his father, who was the minister of her town.

The child, thinking she expected his father to die soon, said: "No, I'll ne'er be minister here. Yonder is my church," and he pointed to the spire of Inveresk, which is not far distant from his native home. This the old woman considered prophesy that the child was foreordained for Inveresk and the people of that parish accepted her interpretation and dared not "quarrel with God's appointed."

ARGYLL'S IDEAS.

A PRESBYTERIAN DUKE'S DEFENSE OF THE BELIEF IN THE MIRACULOUS.

The Duke of Argyll, father of the present Marquis of Lorne,, who is a son-in-law of Queen Victoria, published in 1866 a volume containing a series of papers in support of the belief in miracles. These papers were originally published in various British periodicals but were enlarged and corrected as criticisms of and answers to them appeared from representatives of the various schools of skepticism and materialistic philosophy.

The Duke distinguished himself before he attained his majority as a defender of Scotch Presbyterianism and hence his work on miracles must be regarded as the expression of an orthodox opinion. His book is entitled "The Reign of Law," and so popular does it appear to have been that several editions have been published on both sides of the Atlantic. The first chapter is devoted to the supernatural. In it he says that miracles are really events brought about by the operation of law and he argues very closely to show the reasonableness of this view. He says, page 13:

> Advancing knowledge of physical laws has been accompanied by advancing power over the physical world. It has enabled us to do a thousand things, any

one of which, a few generations ago, would have been considered supernatural.

In this connection he mentions a lecturer on the subject of heat, who exhibited many wonderful things, among them ice frozen in contact with red-hot crucibles. Upon this he remarks:

If the progress of discovery is as rapid for the next 400 years as it has been during the last period of the same extent, men will be able to do many things which would now appear to be supernatural.

* * *

No man can have any difficulty in believing that there are natural laws of which he is ignorant; nor in conceiving that there may be beings who do know them, and can use them even as he himself now uses the few laws with which he is acquainted.

* * *

The relation in which God stands to those rules of His government which are called "laws" is, of course, an inscrutable mystery to us.

The Duke in the course of his definition of terms preparatory to entering upon his arguments quotes approvingly from Dr. Horace Bushnell, whose work is noticed elsewhere:

That is supernatural, whatever it be, that is either not in the chain of natural cause and effect, or which acts on the chain of cause and effect in nature, from without the chain.

After arguing that the spread of Christianity and the preservation of the Jews as a distinct people are the results of Divine interposition, i. e., miracles, he moralizes on the belief in miracles being essential to religion, and says:

Once admit that there is a Being who—irrespective of any theory as to the relation in which the laws of Nature stand to His will—has at least an infinite knowledge of those laws and an infinite power of putting them to use—then miracles lose every element of inconceivability. In respect to the greatest and highest of all—that restoration of the breath of life which is not more mysterious than its original gift—there is no answer to the question which Paul asks: "Why should it be thought a thing incredible by you that God should raise the dead?"

Were I to quote further from Argyll or from those divines whose writings he quotes in support of his position, much matter that has already been written would be repeated and this work be made unnecessarily long. I therefore simply mention the names of a few as James McCosh, LL.D.; Rev J. McLeod Campbell; John Tulloch, D. D., principal of St. Mary's College, St. Andrews, Edinburgh. As the work contains no direct reference to recent miracles, but mentions approvingly Dr. Bushnell's work on that subject, it is fair to construe its arguments as applying to miracles of all times. This construction seems warranted also by a line in the preface to the fifth edition, viz: "The argument it maintains is at variance with the philosophy of some of the most active and popular thinkers of the time; and on a few important points it deviates from the view com-

ARGYLL'S IDEAS. 27

monly adopted by men with whom I am more generally agreed." In two copious notes appended to the volume he answers two of his critics, Dr. Ward, editor of the Dublin Review, and Rev. J. P. Mahaffy, but in neither is the critic shown to have disputed the arguments supporting belief in miracles. In a note appended to page 19 he quotes Rev. J. M. Campbell in support of his theory that miracles are in accordance with law over which God, the infinite author, has infinite control, though these laws and their operation transcend our knowledge.

One who cares to go into minute details of the study of natural laws and trace their wide ramifications will find "The Reign of Law" a most interesting volume aside from its chapter on the supernatural.

His grace quotes the philosopher Locke to the effect that we can never know what is above nature unless we know all that is within nature, and on this he comments:

In this passage Locke * * * * misses another truth, quite as important—that a miracle would still be a miracle even though we did know the laws through which it was accomplished, provided those laws, though not beyond human knowledge, were beyond human control. We might know the conditions necessary to the performance of a miracle although utterly unable to bring those conditions about. Yet a work performed by the bringing about of conditions which are out of human reach would certainly be a work attesting superhuman power.

PURITANS AND MIRACLES.

EVIDENCE OF THE PILGRIM FATHERS' BELIEF THAT GOD INTERVENED IN THEIR BEHALF.

Though a majority, perhaps, of those who claim direct religious descent from the Plymouth pilgrims are the most active in sowing disbelief in miracles, the history of the Pilgrim settlement in Massachusetts contains many acknowledgments of such belief. In 1867 a history of the Pilgrim Fathers was published by the American Tract Society. The author was W. Carlos Martyn, who also wrote a history of the English Puritans. In giving an account of the rise of Puritanism in England Martyn attributes it to zeal with which the Lord touched the hearts of a number of yeomen in the North of England. When describing the voyage to Holland, in 1608, the historian quotes Young, a former historian, to the effect that when the ship was driven by storms to the coast of Norway and was about to be wrecked, God rescued them. Young was on board the ship and his words are thus given:

> But when man's hope and help wholly failed, the Lord's power and mercy appeared for their recovery, for the ship rose again and gave the mariners courage once more to manage her. While the waters ran into their very ears and mouths and all cried, "We sink, we sink," they also said, if not miraculous, yet with great

PURITANS AND MIRACLES. 29

height of Divine faith, "Yet, Lord, thou canst save." And He who holds the winds in His fist and the waters in the hollow of His hand did hear and save them.

Then when the religious adventurers wearied of Holland and decided to try the wilds of America, Martyn says they "announced their intention" to follow Columbus, and launch boldly across the Atlantic, "trusting in God." Having come to this decision they, "after humble prayers unto God for his direction and assistance," held another conference as to what part of America they should decide upon. As they were not in favor with the government and had no hope of obtaining a charter for land, they determined in this, as in other things, to rest on God's providence, but they also rested somewhat in London merchants, who formed a company, got a charter and became partners with the Pilgrims. The terms were hard upon the adventurers, but they accepted them and "had a solemn meeting and a day of humiliation to seek the Lord for his direction."

Martyn closes Chapter VI of his work with a reflection on the singular combination of circumstances which produced the Plymouth settlement, and says:

God builded better than men knew and, when the time was ripe, He chose the Pilgrims, Englishmen, Protestants, exiles for religion, men disciplined by misfortune, cultivated by opportunities of extensive observation, equal in rank as in rights, bound by no code but that of religion and the public will, and with these elements He planted a model state and bade it grow into a democracy, Christian commonwealth, that it might be, at once, an exemplar and a benefactor to mankind.

These extracts are sufficient to show that the Pilgrim fathers in the seventeenth century and the American Tract Society in 1867 believed in miraculous intervention by God in the affairs of mankind. But the Puritans also believed that God intervened in their behalf to save them from starvation, from the treachery of the Indians and from the consequences of the folly and vice of irreligious settlers. On page 198, after moralizing on the futility of the communal experiment of the first two years and its abandonment, Bradford, one of the historians of the colony, is quoted thus:

> Let none object that this is man's corruption and nothing to the philosophy (socialistic) per se. Yes; but since all men have this corruption in them, God, in His wisdom, saw another course fitter for them.

When the colonists finished planting the second year all their food had been consumed, "and they rested on God's providence alone." Wherefore Bradford says, "they above all people in the world had occasion to pray to God to give them their daily bread." After detailing how a scanty supply of food was procured the history shows that just as the colonists were expecting a bounteous corn crop a drouth came and famine threatened.

> In this emergency, the devout Pilgrims resorted to the "mercy seat and besought Him who had so often appeared to succor them to aid them now. A special day of fasting and prayer was appointed."

PURITANS AND MIRACLES.

It has been well said that answers to prayer do not generally come with observation. They are often sent in a way which is hid from most persons and frequently even from those who receive them. There are, however, instances in which these answers are so striking as to be visible to all.

Thus writes Martyn, the modern historian of the American Tract Society, and he follows it up by saying that the fast day opened with a cloudless sky, but he quotes Winslow, another writer from observation, to show that at the close of the services the sky was overcast and a soft rain that began next day continued fourteen days. On this Winslow remarks:

It was hard to say whether our withered corn or our drooping affections were most quickened and revived, such was the bounty and goodness of our God.

God again intervened to defeat a conspirator against the prosperity of the Puritans. One of the merchant adventurers by trickery gained a charter or patent that included all their lands and much more, all in his own name. He set out with a large ship for those days but was twice driven back by storms or defects in his vessel and he "was by this time grown so sick of his patent that he vomited it up."

I have here only quoted from or referred to half of Martyn's history and have not sought to amplify the evidence of Puritan belief in special providence or miracles. I used Martyn's work because it was the most compendious and because it bore the orthodox endorsement I have mentioned.

Not only did these godly men believe that they were miraculously saved from death by wreck, famine and savage warfare and from the machinations of civilized enemies, but that the Lord had depopulated the region to which He guided them. Hutchinson's history says (Vol. I, page 38):

> Our ancestors supposed an immediate interposition of Providence in the great mortality among the Indians, to make room for the settlement of the English.

Palfry, in his history published in 1892, in a note on page 177 of Vol. I, comments on this remark of Hutchinson:

> He who understands that there is a divine government of human affairs, and who recalls what has followed upon the occupation of this region by civilized men, may well hesitate to pronounce that they erred in that belief.

Those who want further evidence that Congregationalists did not always discredit miracles should, beside reading the sketch of the first Puritan settlement in New England, read the biographies of Increase Mather, first president of Harvard College, and his still more widely noted son, Cotton Mather. They believed in other miracles than those for evil and by the power of the devil. They believed themselves to be God-guided and inspired, at least to some extent. That the record Cotton Mather made is disgraceful alike to the church of which he was a minister and to Christianity in no wise militates against the fact that he represented Congregationalist thought in New England in the day in which he lived. And that thought was, when interpreted by the acts of its exponents, that the devil was a great power; that God's power could not be relied on to

PURITANS AND MIRACLES.

counteract it; that man had to oppose his own power to it and stamp it out by murder and cruelties beside which sudden murder was mercy. The only logical deduction is that the followers of Mather thought the devil more powerful than God and themselves more powerful than the devil.

If belief in miracles and belief in witchcraft are both belief in the supernatural, then those who planted the Congregational church on American soil believed in the interposition of supernatural power for evil if they did not believe in it for good. For the purposes of this work this reference is sufficient for this chapter.

On the subject of belief in miracles and treating witchcraft as miraculous, Lecky says in "Rationalism in Europe" that Protestantism "from the beginning looked upon modern miracles (except those which were comprised under the head of witchcraft) with an aversion and distrust that contrasts remarkably with the unhesitating credulity of its opponents." Lecky cites a number of cases that form striking exceptions to the rule of doubt which gradually extended from modern miracles to those of the fathers, after Constantine's conversion. The wave of doubt having been set in motion the theologians found themselves unable to arrest it. Indeed, they seemed to fear that they would be overwhelmed by it, and Lecky says Christianity became an attenuated system of moral philosophy, an admirable auxiliary to the police force.

STARTLING MIRACLES.

AN EMINENT CONGREGATIONALIST DIVINE'S WORK ON DIVINE HEALING.

Among the most eminent and respectable of modern theologians who have written on the subject of miracles is Horace Bushnell. In his work, "Natural and Supernatural," a work of 372 pages, he refers to numerous cases of marvelous cures as late as the present century and some of them in America. Those of ealier day were performed among the Huguenots who fled to England; among the Jansenists in Paris; at St. Medard, in France and by George Fox, the originator of the Quaker sect, but Bushnell, in Fox's cases, omits the dates and other particulars, as if these were too well known to call for further details than that they were performed in Maryland.

The most marvelous thing he relates is a story of Arthur Howell, a Quaker leather currier, who worked in Philadelphia, and who relieved the memory of a deceased woman from the suspicion of a horrible crime, though he had never known the woman in life. Her innocence was revealed to him as her funeral was passing him on the street and he stopped the procession to proclaim what was afterwards abundantly proved. This story is not dated, but it appears on page 325 of "Natural and Supernatural."

Bushnell takes the Christian Observer to task for discredit-

STARTLING MIRACLES.

ing miracles and says it takes substantially the same ground as the atheistic Hume, viz: "We must admit of any solution rather than a miracle." Upon this Dr. Bushnell comments:

Little wonder it is that we have difficulty in sustaining the historic facts of Christianity when the most Christian, the most evangelical teachers, assume so readily the utter incredibility of any such gifts and wonders as the gospels report and as they, themselves, have it for a righteousness to believe.

This is quoted from page 329 and from that to the 346th page he relates several cases of what he terms miraculous cures and solutions of grave difficulties, such as one hears at experience meetings in Christian Scientist churches on Wednesday evenings. Bushnell would not sneer at these relations as do many if not most orthodox clergymen of to-day, though he was a D. D. of the Wesleyan University and an LL.D. of Harvard. It is true that he was accused of heresy in writing his "God in Christ," but he was acquitted by the association of Congregationalist ministers who tried him. He wrote his "Natural and Supernatural" before "Science and Health" was even outlined and it was published in 1858.

In the face of these learned men, who support their opinions by excellent reasonings, the lesser lights of some orthodox churches, to whom Dr. Bushnell should be respectable authority, stigmatize as shallow, ill-trained, ill-brained and fanatical those who believe in the healing power of mind, even with the living evidences before them in the forms of wives, husbands, brothers, sisters, parents and children rescued from the verge of the grave by its agency. Such doubters try to jest fact out of existence to sneer down truth and, by the methods of the stump orator and the police court attorney, to discredit even the words of Him who spake as never man spake.

Methodist Miracles.

EVANGELISTS' TESTIMONY.

METHODIST REVIVALISTS TELL HOW GOD GAVE THEM SPECIAL AID.

That John Wesley, the originator of Methodism, believed in miracles is evident from the history of Methodism by Abel Stevens, D. D., New York and London, 1858. In the earliest pages of the work several events are described from which the inference is unavoidable that the author regards them as of supernatural origin. The "physical phenomena" or "jerks" are attributed to the devil, but the rescue of Wesley when he was a child from his father's house, which was burning, is related as if it were miraculous, though details related show that it was somewhat marvelous yet was well accounted for on purely natural grounds. The tone of the author shows that he regards it as miraculous and this indicates that the belief survived among Methodist doctors of divinity until after the middle of this century.

The physical phenomena were such as were common, and still are, at revivals and camp meetings in some parts of the United States. These Wesley attributed to Satan mimicking God's work, but the historian argues that the primitive Christians "had the jerks" and the early American Presbyterians

EVANGELISTS' TESTIMONY.

were similarly affected at camp meetings, and he fortifies his position by relating numerous wonders of that kind.

WESLEY'S ARGUMENT.

Wesley's argument that miracles are realities is that all Christians believe in a general providence; that there could be no general providence if there were no special providence, because a whole without parts is inconceivable, and that special providences are miracles. In answer to the self-propounded question, "Do you expect miracles?" he answered:

Certainly I do if I believe the Bible; for the Bible teaches me that God hears and answers prayer, but every answer to prayer is properly a miracle. If natural causes take their course, if things go on in their natural way, it is no answer at all.

Rev. Joshua Marsden, an English Wesleyan, after a visit to the United States in 1812, published a sketch of Francis Asbury, one of the early bishops of the Methodist church in this country. In the sketch Mr. Marsden said: "Divine wisdom seemed to direct all his undertakings, for he sought its counsel upon all occasions."

"METHODIST FANATICS."

"A Barrister," in a series of papers on the Evangelical sects, in the London Quarterly Review, Vol. IV (1820), complains of the "bigotry and fanaticism" of the orthodox dissenters and Methodists of that day. He cited their organs, the "Evangelical" and "Methodist" magazines in proof of their human weakness. The Methodist Magazine for October, 1804, declared that the recovery of the King in 1788 was due to the prayers of John Pawson and his congregation, and this was considered proof enough of the charge of fanaticism.

Itinerant preachers of the Methodist church were represented to have had special gifts for causing rain in seasons of drouth, and the magazine is charged with such fanaticism as asserting that the Methodists caused the abatement of a plague of caterpillars by producing an invasion of crows by which the pests were devoured. The barrister quotes quite at length from the magazine named, an article written by William Shepherd of Banbury, who in 1804 claimed to have restored to life a child that had died before medical aid could be summoned. Shepherd wrote that within an hour and a half after he recalled the child's life it had eaten a meal and was playing around the house as if nothing unusual had occurred.

ELDER JACOB KNAPP.

Elder Jacob Knapp, who was to the East what Peter Cartwright was to the Mississippi valley, adds his testimony to the reality of modern miracles, in his autobiography. After relating the difficulties with which he contended during his early days as an evangelist, he says, on page 32:

> But in my distress I cast my burdens on the Lord. I sought to know the will of God. I cried unto the Lord and, blessed be His name, very soon He made known His ways and lifted upon me the light of His countenance. After spending one whole night in fasting and prayer and continuing my fast till midnight, the place where I was staying was filled with the manifested

EVANGELISTS' TESTIMONY. 41

Glory of God. His presence was revealed to me, not exactly in visible form, but as really to my recognition as though He had come in person, and a voice seemed to say to me: "Hast thou ever lacked a field in which to labor?" I answered: "Not a day." "Have I not sustained thee and blessed thy labors?" I answered: "Yea, Lord." "Then learn that henceforth thou art not dependent on thy brethren but upon me. Have no concern, but go on in thy work. My grace shall be sufficient for thee."

I will only make one more reference to Knapp's belief in miracles in his behalf. On page 96 of his book he relates that in February, 1839, in Rochester, N. Y., while snow lay on the ground a mob attacked the church where he was preaching, when a violent thunder storm arose and the lightning's flashes were so vivid that the mob was dispersed.

PETER CARTWRIGHT.

What American has not heard of Peter Cartwright? He was one of the most notable of pioneer preachers of the Methodist church in the then far West. He was licensed as an exhorter in 1802 in Kentucky and was during more than half a century a very prominent figure and powerful propagator of Christianity as expounded by his church. That he believed in miracles is more evident in the preface to his autobiography than complimentary to the modern Methodist. In his preface he says:

MIRACULOUS DULLNESS.

When I consider the unsurmountable disadvantages and difficulties that the early pioneer Methodist preachers labored under in spreading the Gospel in these western wilds, in the great valley of the Mississippi, and contrast the disabilities that surrounded them on every hand, with the glorious human advantages that are enjoyed by their present successors, it is confoundingly miraculous to me that our modern preachers cannot preach better and do more good than they do.

In describing scenes at camp meetings and revivals, Mr. Cartwright tells at some length of "the jerks," a spasmodic affliction, that came upon many who were in attendance. He grows amusing when he describes the humiliation of finely dressed young men and women being seized and the finery of the ladies go flying under the influence of these physical phenomena. One incident which he relates is far from amusing, however, and it is here copied. He does not say just when the tragic event occurred, but as it was soon after he began his ministry it must have occurred not later than 1802. The story is this:

MIRACLE FATAL TO A SCOFFER.

While I am on this subject I will relate a very serious circumstance which I knew to take place with a man who had the jerks at a camp meeting on what was called the ridge, in William Magee's congregation. There was a great work of religion in the encampment. The jerks were very prevalent. There was a company of drunken rowdies who came to interrupt the meeting. These rowdies were headed by a very large drinking man. They came with their bottles of whisky in their pockets. This large man cursed the jerks and all religion. Shortly afterward he took the jerks and he started to run, but he jerked so powerfully he could not get away. He halted among some saplings and, although he was violently agitated, he took out his bottle of whisky and swore he would drink the damned jerks to death, but he jerked at such a rate he could not get the bottle to his mouth, though he tried hard. At length he fetched a sudden jerk, and the bottle struck a sapling and was broken to pieces and spilled his whisky on the ground. There was a great crowd gathered around him, and when he lost his whisky he became very much enraged, and cursed and swore very profanely, his jerks still increasing. At length he fetched a very violent jerk, snapped his neck and soon expired with his mouth full of cursing and bitterness.

Cartwright's comment was this:

I always looked upon the jerks as a judgment sent from God, first, to bring sinners to repentance, and, secondly, to show professors that God could work with or without means and that He could work over and above means and do whatever seemeth Him good, to the glory of His grace and the salvation of the world.

In Chapter IX of Cartwright's autobiography he tells of the hardships he endured in Ohio and in getting back to his father's home in Kentucky for a new outfit; his receipts during a year not being sufficient to pay for a new suit of clothes.

He set out with seventy-five cents, but Providence raised up friends for him on the way and they voluntarily furnished him money. This was in 1807. When he reached Hopkinsville, Ky., he found a tavern kept by an acquaintance of his father and was entertained on credit. During the night the landlord's wife was seized with hysterics and her screams aroused the weary preacher, who rose and asked the cause of the trouble. When it was explained he offered to pray, which offer the afflicted woman eagerly accepted. He prayed and sang and the poor woman, who was described as the sister of an apostate Baptist minister, was healed of her disorder and her husband was overjoyed.

I have here cited only sufficient to show that the venerable preacher who spent his life from early manhood to feeble age in preaching the Gospel according to the Methodist church, agreed with Wesley, its founder, in believing in miracles and special providences, in healing by the invocation of divine aid and in what Christian Scientists now characterize as "demonstrating" for ways and means.

NEWLAND MAFFIT.

Elderly people may remember a great revivalist in Rev. J. Newland Maffit, who from about 1822 to 1848 created great sensations wherever he went. On account of the great scandal that surrounded his latter years and his death, his career is rarely referred to now by Methodists. He was not only the peer of Knapp and Cartwright as an evangelist, but greatly superior to them in education. I have been unable to find any biography of him beyond the brief sketches in encyclopaedias

EVANGELISTS' TESTIMONY. 45

but I am old enough to distinctly remember his visit to my native home and the great sensation it created. I also remember the stories that were current of miraculous conversions and some miraculous occurrences that were hardly religious in their character. The first were related by pious people and of the others only a part were accepted by the pious. I cannot now verify my statements by documentary evidence, but there are many living people who will readily recall what I have here written as fact. The appalling fate that overtook the once brilliant man, whether he was guilty of all that was charged upon him or not, apparently caused most of religious people, orthodox and "liberal" alike, to let his name drop into oblivion if it would. His few writings are now more rare than valuable, I assume, but enough is known of him to show that he and the Methodists of his day believed that miracles were wrought by more than a dozen of their leaders.

Rev. Chauncy Giles published a little book in 1890 on the efficacy of prayer, but he, like many others who believe that prayer is answered, prescribed very minute conditions precedent to be observed. Among them I failed to find healing of illness classed with things that would be "asked amiss," but the reverend author does not make it plain that he regards it as one of the laudable objects of supplication.

JACOB GRUBER.

Jacob Gruber was one of the earliest of Methodist preachers in the Southern States. He was zealous, earnest, vigorous, self-denying, "an unrelenting enemy of ease," and a man of unwavering faith. It is related of him in "Methodist Heroes" that night once overtook him on a mountain during a heavy snow storm and he lost his way. He had to keep moving and close to his horse all night to keep from freezing and when morning came he reached a cabin before the inmates had risen. In response to their congratulations he said the Lord supported him and he didn't even take cold.

Another night he was exposed in a similar manner and in the morning he and his horse safely crossed a dangerous river on the ice. He did not find the house he was seeking until he and his horse had been without food nearly or quite two days, yet again he escaped cold because, he explained, the Lord saved him.

SAM JONES' EXPERIENCE.

THE REVIVALIST RELATES THE HISTORY OF HIS CONVERSION AND FIRST SERMON.

Sam Jones, the great Southern revivalist, opens his autobiography, in his "Own Book," with a quotation from Charles G. Finney and applies it to his own case, viz: "It has pleased God, in some measure, to connect my name and labors with an extensive movement of the church of Christ." This Jones makes more specific on page 15 of that autobiographical sketch. After telling of his dissipation and his promise to his dying father to reform he says:

When peace and pardon were given, after days of seeking, I was impressed that I should preach the Gospel. I did not know from whence these impressions came; I thought as did Gideon Ausely, "I cannot preach, I am not fit to preach, I do not know anything to preach." I sought the advice and counsel of several faithful preachers and I believe each of them said the same thing: "You are called to preach. You can go willingly into it, or you will lose your religion if you refuse. * * * I conferred not with flesh and blood further but began immediately to preach the Gospel as only a man can preach it who knew but two facts—God is good and I am happy in his love.

Jones then tells the story of his first sermon, which, though

PROTESTANT MIRACLES.

he does not say he was inspired, reads like the relation of a miracle. He had gone to an appointment with his grandfather, a preacher, who was hoarse. The preacher who was to have taken the venerable gentleman's place failed to arrive and Grandfather Jones told Sam he must fill the appointment, saying: "If God is calling you to preach, you can preach; come on in the pulpit."

He then describes his opening, but says he has forgotten his exigesis and analysis and says "'hundreds were melted to tears and many went forward for prayers." After service his grandfather assured him that God had called him and bade him go ahead with the work.

Jones has gone ahead and his fame as a revival preacher is equal to, though not of the same kind, as that of Professor Finney, whose case seems to him so much like his own. The thousands who have crowded Sam Jones' meetings in all parts of the United States have heard him relate his own experience and many other stories of miraculous conversions, testify that Protestant sectarians believe in miracles, each within their own sects and in answer to the prayers of their favorite preachers. but each are skeptical concerning those performed through the instrumentality of other evangelists. Especially is this skepticism true as applies to new systems of religion and the advocates thereof.

AN EMINENT METHODIST.

BISHOP FOWLER ON SPECIAL PROVIDENCES WITH EXAMPLES OF MIRACLES.

Charles H. Fowler, D. D. LL.D., is one of the brightest men in the Methodist Episcopal Church, of which he is a bishop. When he was editor of the New York Christian Advocate, a sermon of his special providences was published in the "Complete Preacher" for July, 1877. In that sermon Dr. Fowler said:

It is just as much account to pray about the weather as it was when Elijah prayed about it. Here is a storm beating up the coast likely to drive everything to pieces. The Lord touches somewhere else in the universe some other element, gives it a little turn, and the storm veers off. All we need is to get hold of the great combiner. A Baptist preacher by the name of Edwards, who had been an old sea captain,* when a a tornado was coming straight down upon his house, knew that there was mischief in the cloud. He believed that God was at home in Wisconsin, and calling to his children said: "Do you see that cloud? That means harm. Let us go into the house and tell God about it." And they went in and prayed to the Lord that he would

---

* The Edwards here is undoubtedly the person referred to elsewhere as having been mysteriously supplied with groceries and fuel.

take care of them if they were worth saving. They were saved and the next day and for months afterwards you could see the broad track of that tornado that cleaned up every blade of grass, every roof and hamlet, and tree and stick and stump in its path, bearing right down on this clergyman's house until it came within a quarter of a mile of it, when it made an abrupt turn, went to one side till opposite his house, then it turned back into its old path and went on. That man got hold of the great Combiner and the Lord looked after him.

Dr. Fowler illustrated his idea by a hypothetical case. He supposed a pious man in deep meditation over whose path hung a tree that was liable to fall any moment. A sound arrests his footsteps in time to prevent him being under the tree as it falls, "and he is as much saved by the providence of God as he would have been if the Lord had come out and rolled up his sleeves and held up the tree before the eyes of men.

He cited the case of a soldier who was moved by an irresistible impulse to get under cover while eating his lunch one day in front of Petersburg. He had hardly moved his head when a rebel bullet pierced the tree where it had rested. On this he comments: "He was saved as much as if the Lord had come down and turned aside that gun."

He also recited the case of a ship's return to her home port after a three years' voyage and, as she was about to land her crew, a storm sent her upon the rocks, where she was pounded to pieces. A poor woman who had been to the shore to meet her son went home and spent the night in prayer. At daylight

AN EMINENT METHODIST.

that son burst into the room and cried: "I knew, mother, that you would pray me ashore." Upon this Fowler said: "She, too, got hold of the great Combiner. That is what I believe about Providence and about prayer, and the Bible is full of it from one end to the other."

Dr. Fowler did not stop there. He told of Fletcher being saved to the church and to God by the act of a clumsy servant scalding him and thus preventing him going to sea as a lieutenant in the British navy in a ship that never came back.

MIRACLES THAT ENTERTAIN.

STORIES OF GOD'S INTERVENTION IN AID OF THE STRIVERS AFTER VIRTUE.

Rev. J. V. Watson, D. D., was a man who was deeply respected in the morning and until the noon of the present century, when he died. He entered the itinerant ministry of the Methodist Episcopal Church during the second decade of the century and was for many years editor of the Northwestern Christian Advocate, in Chicago. After his death a book he had in preparation was published and, though all the articles it contains were not written by him, the author said the staple of the volume was from his pen and, as all of it was culled from the paper of which he was for ten years the editor, the miraculous incidents must be regarded as having the stamp of Methodist approval.

The story with which Dr. Watson opens his volume has for its chief incidents the inspiration of a young preacher and the resultant conversion of his scoffing brother. It was written by a woman whose name is not given, except as "Sister A." Elliott Ray is the young preacher who, on attempting to preach while his taunting brother sat facing him and ready to execute a threat, failed for a moment. Then, knowing that his mother was at home praying for his success, he began by beseeching those present to pray also and, through his mother's prayers, grew more and more eloquent until the whole congre-

MIRACLES THAT ENTERTAIN.

gation was profoundly moved, many to tears and the sneering brother Charles converted.

The ninth story is by Sylvanus Cobb, probably not the author once so well known with the addition of "junior" to his name, but his father, who was an honored clergyman. It tells of the almost miraculous reclamation of a besotted father who awoke from a half drunken sleep in a patch of woods and overheard his little daughter bewailing his degradation and contrasting it with his former loving kindness and provident care for them and discussing their mother's ardent prayers for his reform. It is a prettily written story and closes with the acknowledgment of the husband that his wife's prayers are answered.

"The Unwelcome Preacher" contains a much more striking miracle story. It is an account of a Kentucky village that contained twenty-seven self-important Methodists, who, in 1823, asked for the most noted and popular preacher of the state as their pastor. The conference sent them a young man who had just been admitted to the conference and who was, in consequence, so very coldly received, that his heart would have failed him had not Bishop George accompanied him.

The young man pleaded to have the appointment cancelled, but the bishop conducted him into a deep wood, where they both prayed for success. This helped the youth, because the bishop had fallen ill while they were on the journey to the station. The bishop, after failing to prevail upon the youth to try to cure him by prayer, resorted to supplication for himself, and was healed. Here is miracle No. 1 of this story,

PROTESTANT MIRACLES.

which is a mere incident of the narrative. After the prayer in the woods the bishop exacted a promise from the young man to follow this prescription:

> Go back to town; if you find a cross there bear it; diligently and lovingly perform every part of your duty; do the work of an evangelist; fast once a week, and spend one hour of each day in special prayer that God may open your way in that community; do this for one month and at the end of that term, if you do not feel willing to stay, consider yourself released from the appointment. Can you do this?

He thought he could, and the bishop left him and pursued his journey, leaving the half fainting youth to God and His mercy. Faithfully was the promise kept without sign of any change until the last Sunday of his probation. When he peeped out on the morning of that day the roads showed "group after group of citizens flocking toward the Methodist church." The sight was naturally inspiring and the author of the story describes the sermon as that of "a man sent from God" and gloriously baptized with the Holy Ghost and that his eye, hitherto confused and unsteady, "now kindled with a light that never shined on sea or shore.'" He adds:

> The power of the Highest was manifestly upon the audience and the presence of an ambassador of Christ was attested by sobs and groans from every part of the house. The preacher descended from the pulpit without pausing in his discourse, and invited to the place of prayer those who desired to flee the wrath to come.

MIRACLES THAT ENTERTAIN.

With loud cries for mercy, sinners came streaming down the aisle and before the congregation was dismissed seven souls professed to find peace in believing.

This was followed by a revival which for four weeks was so all-absorbing that little else received any attention. When the call was made for those who wished to join the church one hundred and eleven presented themselves.

That village was made a permanent station and the author discloses in two brief paragraphs at the conclusion of his story that it is Russellville, Ky., and that the unwelcome preacher was then (in 1856) Rev. E. Stevenson, D. D., book agent of the M. E. Church South.

Dr. Watson did one praiseworthy act in getting out his book. He devoted a chapter to Newland Maffit and in it displays sufficient Christian charity to touch lightly on the offenses charged on that gifted but erratic zealot and give him full credit for what of good was in him.

ORTHODOX PRAYER CURE.

A TEXT BOOK FOR METHODIST PREACHERS WHICH TEACHES MIRACULOUS HEALING.

Rev. James Caughey, who is described as "an eminently successful revivalist" on the title page of a work with the lengthy title, "Helps to a Life of Holiness and Usefulness or Revival Miscellanies," contributes a striking bit of evidence in support of religion as a cure for disease. That his works must be regarded as authority, I accept as evidence that the matter in the volume from which I shall quote was "selected" by Rev. Ralph W. Allen and Rev. Daniel Wise and was of the forty-second thousand. On page 345 of this work Mr. Caughey speaks of an "ingenius Dr. C." thus:

> Dr. C. reckons all gloomy wrong-headedness and spurious free-thinking as so many symptoms of bodily disease and, I think, says: "The human organs in some nervous distempers may, perhaps, be rendered fit for the actuation of demons" and advises religion as an excellent remedy.

In a chapter devoted to answers to prayer two pages, 401 and 402, are devoted especially to the subject. The writer quotes a simile employed by others who had spoken and written before him, which likened the petitioner to a man in a boat who grappled a ship. The ship did not yield to him but towed the boat with it. Of this Mr. Caughey says:

ORTHODOX PRAYER CURE.

I do not like the idea, however ingeniously carried out, that God is as stationary, with regard to the returning sinner or praying believer, as the ship to the boatman. It seems to make against the analogy of the Scripture, "Draw nigh to God and He will draw nigh to you. James, iv:8. This seems like a proposal to meet us half way, and if we take the example of the prodigal son, as illustrative of the willingness of God to receive returning sinners, our Heavenly Father performs the largest part. The prodigal did not run to meet his father but his father ran to meet the repenting son, "and fell upon his neck and kissed him."

In a chapter devoted to preaching the author tells a story that would have fitted well into that from which the foregoing extract was taken. It is in brief that a young minister named Stoddard, at Northhampton, Mass., whose congregation became convinced that he had never been converted because, though he was learned and devoted to his work, his preaching did not appeal to them. After a conference they decided to hold a meeting at which to pray for his conversion. The pastor, surprised at a gathering of which he had no notice, inquired the cause of one whom he saw going to the church. When informed he retired and prayed for himself. Mr. Caughey says:

> While they were yet speaking, God answered and set His soul at liberty. It was not long before the people of God obtained evidence, most unquestionable, that he had indeed passed "from death unto life." That

man labored among them nearly half a century, and, it is said, he was ranked among the most able ministers of the age.

That Caughey's works are soundly orthodox is evident from the preface, a note which says that after 10,000 copies had been sold in about a year, the plates were purchased by the book agents of the Methodist Episcopal Church South, by whom the book was afterwards published.

COMMUNED WITH GOD.

REVIVALIST CAUGHEY'S ACCOUNT OF HIS FAILURE TO MARRY.

Rev. James Caughey, who is mentioned elsewhere in this volume, as the author of "Revival Miscellanies," was one of the early Methodist preachers in the United States, having been ordained deacon in 1834 at the annual conference in Troy, N. Y. In a biographical sketch in "Earnest Christianity" his words are quoted concerning his communion with God. For the sake of saving space I reduce them to their essence, but those who wish to verify my work or dispute it will find the matter on pages 12 to 15 of the work named, which was edited by Rev. Daniel Wise and Rev. Ralph W. Allen.

In 1839 Mr. Caughey was appointed to Whitehall, N. Y., and began to reflect on taking a wife. Immediately his heart became hard and "the Lord seemed to depart from" him. The more he reflected on the subject the further the Lord seemed to withdraw from him. He says:

> God, who had honored me with such intimate communion with Himself since my conversion, apparently left me to battle it out alone. I was about to step out of the order of His providence and He was resolved to prevent it unless I should refuse to understand why He thus resisted me. Had I continued the conflict I believe He would have let me take my own

course, nor would He have cast me off, yet I solemnly feel He would have severely chastised my disobedience.

While in this state of mind Caughey resorted to fervent and long continued prayer for relief from the weight that oppressed him and light as to what he should do, determined to obey the divine command. He says:

> During three days I cried to God without any answer. On the third day in the afternoon I obtained an audience with the Lord. The place was almost as still as Sinai * * * I left the place without receiving any light, but my heart was fully softened and subdued and I felt sure I had prevailed in some way with God. I was confident light and direction were coming.

On the same evening (July 9, 1839) a light reached him and he gives the following as a feeble attempt to reproduce the form in which the divine will was communicated to him:

> These matters that trouble thee must be let entirely alone. The will of God is that thou shouldst visit Europe. He shall be with thee there and give thee many seals to thy ministry. He has provided thee with funds. Make thy arrangements accordingly; and next conference ask liberally from the proper authorities and it shall be granted thee.

The message also contained some directions how to proceed, and Caughey says it came in a way that left no room for doubt. Throughout the page he tells of the heavenly feelings it left with him, of joy, of rest, of peace, and he exclaims:

COMMUNED WITH GOD. 61

Oh the sweetness of that communication I then enjoyed with God.

The next day he unpacked his books, set his study in order and proceeded to fulfill his pastoral mission and prepare for his coming voyage. The meaning of the expression: "He has provided thee with funds," is explained by saying he had a few hundred dollars, the propriety of accumulating which he had long doubted, but this revelation had cleared his conscience and "the meaning of many past providences was now explained."

In pursuance of the Divine will Caughey obtained leave from the conference; went through Canada as commanded and converted about four hundred persons. Comparatively little is said in the sketch of his work in England, but he created a profound sensation in Dublin, whither he went unannounced. In the seven years of his stay in Ireland and England 22,000 persons professed conversion under his labors.

The body of the work consists of extracts from Caughey's journal. In it can be found many incidents of a miraculous character, but to reproduce them, even in the most abbreviated form, would occupy space unprofitably. They would simply become cumulative evidence of Methodist belief in miracles, which is abundantly proved without them.

Evidence of Baptists.

BAPTIST TESTIMONY.

FATHERS OF THAT DENOMINATION RELATE THE WORKING OF MIRACLES.

The history of the Baptist Church shows that its organization in Holland was miraculous. J. M. Cramp, D. D., in "Baptist History," a work published in London in 1871, quotes from Menno Simon's "Narrative of His Secession From Popery" how he was called upon, about 1535, by several Anabaptists who besought him to become their pastor. He did not deem himself qualified because, though he had been several years a Catholic priest, he was not sufficiently familiar with the Scriptures. His callers were urgent, however, and he says:

At length, after much prayer, I resigned myself to the Lord and His people with this condition: They were to unite with me in praying to Him fervently, that, should it be His holy pleasure to employ me in His service to His praise, His fatherly kindness would then give me such a heart and mind as would testify to me with Paul. "Woe is me if I preach not the Gospel," but should His will be otherwise, that He would order such means as to permit the matter to rest where it was.

In support of this course he quotes Matt. xviii:19,20. It is left to be inferred that the Lord gave Menno the sign he sought, for he became the great leader, and Mossheim says he

BAPTIST TESTIMONY. 65

became "almost the common father and bishop of all the Anabaptists."

Menno has given a name to one sect of Baptists who are widely scattered over Europe and have large settlements in the northwestern States of America. They are known as Mennonites, and those who have settled in the United States are largely emigrants who fled from Russia on the withdrawal of the exemption from military service. They are essentially Germans, their forefathers having left the fatherland on account of oppression and induced by the Czar's promise of perpetual exemption from military duty.

A TRAITOR STRICKEN DUMB.

Menno's success in Holland attracted the attention of the authorities, who persecuted the Baptists and offered a reward for the apprehension of Menno. A traitor agreed, for a reward, to cause the arrest of the apostle at a meeting, but he escaped. Soon afterward Menno, in a boat, passed the traitor and the officers who sought him, on the canal, but the traitor was unable to speak and betray him. When Menno had escaped to the bank the traitor's tongue was loosened and he cried out that the bird had flown. The officers were so incensed that they, disregarding his plea that his tongue had been bound, caused him to be severely punished.

A MINISTER HEALED.

In 1638 Hanserd Knollys, an ordained minister who had abandoned the Church of England after preaching several years, emigrated to New England. He was not allowed to remain in Boston because he was suspected not to be an orthodox

Puritan and he returned to London late in 1640 and sustained himself by teaching while preaching to the Baptists gratuitously. While in America he sojourned at Dover and it is presumably at that place that he was healed of a grave ailment by prayer. Knollys' account of his illness and recovery is this:

Two learned, well-practiced and judicious doctors of physic had daily visited me and consulted several days together, and I was fully persuaded that they did what they possibly could to effect a cure and knew also that God did not succeed their honest and faithful endeavors with His blessing. Although God had given a signal and singular testimony of His special blessing by each of them unto other of their patients, at least sixteen, at the same time, I resolved to take no more physic, but would apply to that holy ordinance of God, appointed by Jesus Christ, the great physician of value, in James v:14,15: "Is any sick among you let them call the elders of the church and let them pray over him, annointing him with oil in the name of the Lord; and the prayer of faith shall save the sick, and the Lord shall raise him up; and if he have committed sins they shall be forgiven him,"— and I sent for Mr. Kiffin and Mr. Vavasor Powell, who prayed over me and annointed me with oil in the name of the Lord. The Lord did hear prayer and heal me; for there were many Godly ministers and gracious saints that prayed day and night for me (with submission to the will of God) that the Lord would spare my life and make me more serviceable to His church and to His saints, whose prayers God heard; and as an answer to their prayers I was perfectly healed but remained weak long after.

The cautious historian in quoting this account of the ancient belief in the power of prayer in healing illness, says: "We copy it without comment," but the miraculous escape of Menno through the informer being deprived of the power of speech, and the Divine evidence of his fitness to become a pastor, was given without the saving clause.

In reviewing his own history some years before his death, Mr. Knollys, who had acquired considerable property after his return to England, wrote:

Thus my Heavenly Father made up my former losses with His future blessings, even in outward substance, besides a good increase of grace and experience, in the space of the forty years that I and my dear faithful wife lived together.

Mr. Knollys died in his ninety-third year and so much was he venerated by Baptists that in 1845 the "Hanserd Knollys Society" was formed for the republication of the works of early Baptist authors. He was among the first three ministers of his denomination in England who were "honored while living and whose memory is blessed."

HE HEALS ANOTHER PREACHER.

Knollys' faith in the power of prayer to heal was not confined in its operative effect to himself. The history from which I quote says, on page 389, that Benjamin Keach, another of the three immortals mentioned above, who was of a weak constitution, was so ill in 1689 that his life was despaired of.

His physicians had exhausted their skill and his relatives took leave of him, expecting his departure to be near at hand, when, as Crosby relates, "The Reverend Mr. Hanserd Knollys, seeing his friend and brother near to all appearances expiring, betook himself to prayer, and, in an earnest and very extraordinary manner, begged that God would spare him and add unto his days the time granted unto His servant Hezekiah. As soon as he had ended his prayer he said: "Brother Keach, I shall be in Heaven before you" and quickly left him. So remarkable was the answer of God to this good man's prayer, that I cannot omit it; though it may be discredited by some, there are yet living incontestable evidences of the fact;— for Mr. Keach recovered of that illness and lived just fifteen years afterwards; and then it pleased God to visit him with that short sickness which put an end to his life." He died July 18, 1704, in the sixty-fourth year of his age.

William Kiffin, the third of the trio, wrote his own memoirs from which Cramp copies copiously. He does not recount any remarkable miracles, but all through the extract copied by Cramp there are acknowledgments that God guided and protected him in the exercise of his religious duties as a minister, teacher and exemplar of the faith.

A REVIVALIST'S MIRACLES.

When I began this work I had little idea that I should find so much material from non-Catholic authorities. Before hav-

BAPTIST TESTIMONY.

ing made any researches I had almost accepted the dicta of my Protestant friends and those authorities whose works I had casually examined, that Protestants agreed that the age of miracles had passed and that God did not now interpose in human affairs because it was not necessary where His word was before mankind to read, learn and believe. I had heard revivalists tell of wonderful things that had happened to them but didn't recall them. One of these stories will serve as a fair sample. A Baptist preacher who was widely known in the "early fifties" as Sailor Edwards said in one of his discourses in Detroit, Mich., that God had commanded him to go forth and rouse a dying people to their danger of everlasting punishment. His wife, of less faith than he, told him he would do better to earn something to eat and something to cook it with. He hearkened to God, rather than to his wife, and though his larder—or what stood in its stead—was empty, he obeyed the command. He learned on his return from his revival tour that he had not been gone an hour when a wagon was driven to his home with ample provisions and was soon followed by a load of stove-wood. He declared that the Lord sent the provisions and fuel and that he had never discovered the human agency employed by the giver of all good. If this miracle was ever disputed I never heard of it. Edwards' home, if my memory serves me correctly, was then at or near Laporte, Indiana, which was, at the time when Edwards flourished, but little less easy to reach than now, and if he did not speak the truth he could easily have been refuted had any cared to make investigation, but I never heard of any being made. In the article on Bishop Fowler of the M. E. Church, elsewhere in this volume, will be found another miracle that saved Edwards' home and family from destruction.

Any person who reads the life or sermons of Spurgeon, the eminent Baptist preacher of London, must conclude that he believed in miracles. His story of the building of the tabernacle and of the Stockwell orphanage plainly indicate the belief in Divine interposition in aid of both those great and laudable enterprises.

ROGER WILLIAMS' TESTIMONY.

Roger Williams, who settled Rhode Island, after being expelled from Massachusetts by the Puritans, bears testimony to the reality of miracles. On that terrible winter night when he was warned to leave the Puritan colony and was refused even the privilege of awaiting the abatement of the storm, a mysterious messenger called on him; gave him minute directions how and whence to proceed. The pious pioneer Baptist followed the directions thus mysteriously given with unfaltering faith that God had sent the unknown, unrecognized stranger. Even when the howling of wolves in the wilderness was such as would have terrified one less steadfast, the outcast Baptist remembered that he was under the protection of God who saved Daniel from the lions and he quailed not.

The history of Roger Williams, his rebukes of what he deemed Puritan sins, his expulsion from Massachusetts and his founding the Baptist colony in Rhode Island, are too well known to need citations of authorities here.

SPURGEON ON PRAYER.

THE EMINENT PREACHER GIVES REASONS FOR BELIEVING IT IS ANSWERED.

Spurgeon, the phenomenal preacher of London, was a firm believer in the power of prayer and that God answered prayers. In one of his "Sermon Notes" (Vol. II, page 162) he says the Lord will answer prayer because:

1. He has appointed prayer and made arrangements for its presentation and acceptance. He could not have meant it to be a mere farce: that were to treat us as fools.

2. He prompts, encourages and quickens prayer; and surely He would never mock us by exciting desires which He never meant to gratify. Such a thought well nigh blasphemes the Holy Ghost who indites prayer in the heart.

Spurgeon gives three other reasons that are scarcely less forcible, the third of which is: "He has already answered many of his people and ourselves also." In fortifying his position he comments on an illustration: "If true prayer is not answered the nature of God must have changed." In support of his position he quotes from Trapp, Thomas Brooks and Harrington Evans.

One cannot read Spurgeon's four volumes of "Sermon

Notes" without being convinced that the author believed that God intervened in human affairs as much as He ever did in answer to prayer and to promote the cause of piety and justice, but the word "miracles" is avoided while miraculous intervention is taught.

College Professors' Teachings.

UNION SEMINARY.

SOME VIEWS FROM THE DIVINITY SCHOOL OF THE PRESBYTERIANS.

The Religious Encyclopaedia, edited by Philip Schaff, D. D. LL.D., professor in Union Theological Seminary in New York, with Rev. Samuel M. Jackson and Rev. D. S. Schaff as associate editors, ought to be accepted as good orthodox authority. It devotes a large amount of space to miracles. In one article by F. Godet occur these passages:

> There is an objection often made to the miracles of Bible history, that none are wrought now. * * *
> The alleged decrease in the series of miracles is absolutely false.

These passages are widely separated, but they apply to the same subject or they have no application.

Julius Kostlin follows Godet in an article on the historical view of miracles, in which he says Luther regarded them as angelic ministrations and set no limits on the agency, yet believed that since Christ came they were not necessary, but he makes no mention of Luther's belief in the supernatural to the extent of causing him to dash a bottle of ink at the devil, who, he said, appeared in his study. The ink mark on the wall was long an object of half-worship by tourists in Germany, who deemed a tour of Europe incomplete if they did not see the splash. After describing the views of several theologians and philosophers on the subject, Kostlin says:

But in truth there are miracles which cannot be explained upon ground of laws inherent in nature. They are only explicable on the supposition of Divine direct action upon nature.

* * *

Before the last word can be spoken upon miracles some definite idea must be attached to the phrase "laws of nature." It will require a more comprehensive treatment of the subject than the scientists are inclined to give it, for much more than material nature must be studied.

CURES AND CONVERSIONS.

DR. BRUCE DEFENDS MODERN MIRACLES IN TWO COLLEGES.

A. M. Bruce, D. D., and professor of apologetics in the Free Church College of Glasgow, Scotland, published in 1893 a volume entitled, "The Miraculous Element in the Gospels." On page 316 he begins the consideration of modern miracles thus:

> How has it come to pass that the whole Christian people, speaking broadly, has allowed the healing of the body to fall into abeyance in comparison with the saving of the soul?

He then says some now think that if the church lived up to Christ's teachings cures would be as common now as conversions. He cites Matt. viii :17; Mark xvi :17 and 18, which some hold to be an unrestricted promise to believers in all ages and says (page 317) that the possibility of supernatural cures in answer to prayer is believed by all who pray, and continues:

> Neither is it a question as to the reality of alleged faith cures, whether of the present or any past time. A Christian man has no interest in obstinately denying their reality. On the contrary, he can only hope that all cases of the kind are as the most enthusiastic ad-

CURES AND CONVERSIONS.   77

vocates of modern miracles could desire, and devotedly wish that their number were greatly multiplied.

Dr. Bruce then relates what misery he witnessed during his apprenticeship as a preacher in Scotland when he longed for the healing power of the apostles. Notwithstanding these declarations Dr. Bruce thinks the church should not put healing on a level with the pardon of sin because "it unduly magnifies the benefit of mere physical health."

Lest the orthodox skeptic concerning what is termed miraculous healing may regard Dr. Bruce as less than full orthodox, it is well to explain, as he does, that his book is a series of lectures prepared at the invitation of Union Theological Seminary of New York, in 1886. In these lectures one is devoted to "Miracles in Relation to the Order of Nature." In this he defends miracles and treats as flimsy the opinions of those who regard them as being in conformity with "higher law" or "unknown law," which he treats as substantially the same thing, or perhaps it would be more descriptive to say, "unsubstantially the same nothing." Dr. Bruce quotes from Matthew Arnold's "Literature and Dogma" thus:

CHRISTIAN SCIENCE ENDORSED.

Medical science has never gauged, perhaps never enough set itself to gauge the intimate connection between moral fault and disease. To what extent or in how many cases what is called illness is due to moral springs having been used amiss, whether by being over-used or by not being used sufficiently, we hardly at all enquire and we too little know. Certainly it is due to this very much more than we commonly think, and the more it is due to this the more do moral therapeutics rise in possibility and importance.

Thereupon Dr. Bruce comments:

On this view it is conceivable that medical science may yet penetrate the secret of Christ's healing ministry, just as it is possible, and we may hope probable, that the causes and cures of such fatal disease as cholera and consumption will yet be discovered. When that day comes moral therapeutics will be a recognized branch of medical art and many of the evangelical "miracles" of healing will be miracles no longer, but natural cures.

After further reasoning to the same effect this learned divine treats of modern instances of apparent miracles and says they are not be taken for granted nor scornfully denied.

Some of the hypotheses advanced by skeptics and so-called liberal Christians to account for miraculous occurrences by physical laws, or on other grounds than those of what are called supernatural theories, are amusing. One of these, which Dr. Bruce notices, is by Paulus, a theological writer. It goes beyond the absurd and attributes deceit to the Savior. It is that Jesus, desiring to make a present to the bridal couple at Cana, Galilee, gave them wine and made them believe he had changed it from water, taking advantage of the company as "na fu' but just had plenty." Others have attributed to Jesus hypnotic powers of such extent as to make the whole bridal company drink water and believe it to be superior wine.

VIEWS FROM YALE.

PROFESSORS FISHER AND HARRIS BELIEVE IN MIRACLES AS REALITIES.

George P. Fisher, professor of church history in Yale University, is the author of a work entitled, "Supernatural Origin of Christianity," published in 1887. He devotes a chapter of fourteen pages to Christian miracles and argues the reasonableness of belief in all except those classed as Catholic. By a course of reasoning, that he fails to see is as forcible against all belief in miracles as against any, seems to satisfy himself that there was no necessity for the Catholic miracles and hence that they were not real.

Fisher does not seem to have remained fixed in this opinion. In his other work, "Grounds of Theistic and Religious Belief," page 291, he evinces a belief in the power of prayer to heal sickness. He says:

> The restoration of the sick in response to prayer is commonly through no visible or demonstrable interference with natural law. Yet no one would be charged with incredulity for holding that, in certain exceptional instances, the supernatural agency discovers itself by evidence palpable to the senses. So discreet an historian as Neander will not deny that St.

Bernard may have been the instrument of effecting cures properly miraculous.

Dr. Fisher quotes Edmund Burke's opinion that in the introduction of Christianity into Britain, by Augustine and his associates, that Providence might have directly interfered for an end so worthy. He also quotes thus from F. D. Maurice:

> I should think it very presumptuous to say that it has never been needful, in the modern history of the world, to break the idols of sense and experience by the same method which was sanctioned in the days of old.

Dr. Fisher makes it plain that he is not credulous on the subject of answers to prayer. On page 292 he says the most that can be said of miracles in post-apostolic ages is that sometimes they have occurred in answer to prayer and he italicizes "sometimes."

PROFESSOR HARRIS A BELIEVER.

The Philosophic Basis of Theism is a work by Samuel Harris, D. D., LL.D., professor of systematic theology in the Yale University, published in 1888. In this the author, pp. 65 to 72, controverts Hume's assertion that a miracle is incredible because contrary to universal experience. Dr. Harris' reasoning is very close, analytical and exhaustive, and his conclusion is that Hume's position is illogical, but the professor does not carry his argument so far as to apply it to any class of miracles. For this reason I assume that it applies as well to modern as to ancient mysteries.

VIEWS FROM YALE.

A VENERABLE YALE MAN.

The venerable Noah Porter, who was for many years a member of the faculty of Yale University, published a volume entitled, "Fifteen Years in the Chapel of Yale College." In that volume is a sermon in which he advises the graduating class of 1881, "Seek ye first the kingdom of God." In the closing words of the sermon he says God "never fails to give success to the man that seeks first whatsoever is true; whatsoever is honorable; whatsoever is lovely; whatsoever is of good report."

AN AMERICAN WAR MIRACLE.

The venerable Timothy Dwight, once president of Yale and for many years tutor and professor in that college, in his lectures on theology teaches that blessings are often given in answer to prayer. If he knew of no other, he says:

> The blessings communicated to this country would furnish ample satisfaction concerning this subject to every sober, much more, to every pious inhabitant of This country. Among these the destruction of the French armament under the Duke D'Auville in the year 1746, ought to be remembered with gratitude and admiration. * * * This fleet consisted of forty ships of war; was destined for the destruction of New England; was of sufficient force to render that destruction, in the ordinary progress of things, certain; sailed from Chebucto, in Nova Scotia, for this purpose, and was entirely destroyed on the night following a general fast throughout New England by a terrible tempest. Im-

pious men, who regard not the work of the Lord, nor the operation of His hands, and who for that reason are finally destroyed, may refuse to give God the glory of this most merciful interposition. But our ancestors had, and it is hoped their descendants ever will have, both piety and good sense, sufficient to ascribe to Jehova the greatness and the power, and the victory, and the majesty; and to bless the God of Israel forever and ever.

The Scriptures put this subject out of doubt by declaring directly, that blessings are given to mankind in answer to prayer.

President Dwight then proceeds to explain that prayer does not change the intentions of the deity or that prayer deserves to be granted, but that "without prayer the blessings would never be obtained."

This ascribes to God all power, but many of those who profess the same religion as President Dwight, while admitting that his teachings are correct, would deny that God could or would relieve suffering humanity of so much as a toothache, however sincerely the sufferer might pray.

DISCREDITS HIMSELF.

WHITE, THE PHILOSOPHER, EDUCATOR AND DIPLOMAT, PERPETUATES ABSURDITIES.

Andrew D. White, former president of Cornell University, present ambassador near the imperial German Court, in the Popular Science Monthly of May, 1891, discredits miracles in an article that is largely devoted to Xavier, who is more generally known as St. Francis Xavier. White says, after illustrating how miracle stories grow, that testimony which would now be laughed at by a school-boy, "was until a comparatively recent period, accepted by the leaders of thought." After exerting his powers of logic to destroy all belief in miracles the eminent educator, philosopher and diplomat thus betrays that he does not fully concur in his own opinion:

It should be especially kept in mind that, while the vast majority of these—(miracle stories)—were doubtless due to the myth-making faculty and to that development of legends which always goes on in ages ignorant of the relation, physical cause and effect, some of the miracles of healing may have had some basis of fact

The learned gentleman seems not to perceive that this admission estops him from further arguing against the reality of what are called miracles, and he continues his effort to put limits on the omnipotent or even on the operation of laws of which even he is ignorant, and at the same time to admit the reality of some miracles, in these words:

We of modern times have seen too many cures performed through influences exercised on the imagination, such as those of the Jansenites at the cemetery of Medard; of the Ultramontanes at Le Sallet and Lourdes and of various Protestant sects—at Old Orchard and elsewhere, as well as at sundry camp-meetings, to doubt that some cures, more or less permanent, were wrought by sainted personages in the early church and throughout the middle ages.

One is prompted to ask where the learned gentleman would draw the line of the limit upon the power of the Almighty to operate laws of His own making, the effect and even the existence of which President White has not been able to trace. If such cures could be effected by saintly or sainted personages in the early church, the power must be extinct or saintly personages must be able to exercise it now. If the power ever existed it was a Divine power and must exist still, or if the learned philosopher imagines it to be extinct it would follow that God must have lost some of His power. Is this what these learned men mean when they attempt to draw the line or trocha, chronologically or geographically, beyond which miracles shall not pass?

The purpose of Dr. White's paper is to discredit all who pretend to heal disease by any other agency than that of drugs

DISCREDITS HIMSELF.

or the surgeon's instruments. He quotes freely from Saints Cyril, Ambrose and Augustine to the effect that "the precepts of medicine are contrary to celestial science, watching and prayer" and says this doctrine was reiterated from time to time throughout the middle ages.

This shows pretty well for Christian Science as a return to the faith and practice of the Christians of the days when Christianity was practiced for its intrinsic virtue, truth and its benefit to humanity. That Dr. White's object is to protect medical practice is further evinced by an article in the succeeding number of the same magazine on the absurd idea that the touch of royal personages cured scrofula and epilepsy. As if to emphasize his contempt for his own opinion that his other opinion was subject to doubt and exception, he says:

> There are no miracles of healing in the history of the human race more thoroughly attested than those wrought by the touch of Henry VIII, Elizabeth, the Stuarts and especially that chosen vessel, Charles II.

These were not all despised Catholic miracles with which White contradicts himself, but he cites others performed in France which were by Catholic monarchs. He also cites other English Protestant cases and then repeats his doubts of himself by quoting from Collier's Ecclesiastical History, that to despise these cases "is to come to the extreme of skepticism, to deny our senses and be incredulous even to ridiculousness."

Notwithstanding the absurd appearance this gives to Prof. White's papers, they are grave in tone and his contradictory positions are sufficiently wide-separated for the inconsistencies to escape the notice of a reader who is not critical.

In a note to his chapter on "Miracles and Medicine," when republished in book form, in 1896, President White relates that on his arrival in St. Petersburg in 1893, to take up his official residence as minister, he heard much of the stories of Father Ivan's miracles. He relates two of these only to follow them by a complete and satisfactory refutation, but also quotes the witness by whom he refutes the two stories as saying that Ivan had done wonders in healing the sick and relieving distress. Upon this White says it was made evident that Ivan is a saintlike man.

Professor John Fiske of Harvard in his book, the "Unseen World," in discussing the errors of scientists in dealing with mystic subjects, says, page 129: "Most scientific and philosophical works have their defects." This remark of the learned educator would apply with peculiar force to that other eminent educator and diplomat, Andrew D. White.

A GERMAN PROFESSOR.

DR. CHRISTLIEB OF BONN UNIVERSITY ON MODERN MIRACLES.

Among those orthodox theologians who dissent from the prevailing opinion or the opinion that is most frequently found recorded in books, is Dr. Theodore Christlieb, professor of theology and university preacher at Bonn, Germany, who was for some years pastor of an orthodox German congregation in London. He delivered a series of lectures, some of them in London on the subject of miracles and these were published in book form in 1874 under the title: "Modern Doubt and Christian Belief." The first four lectures are devoted to the miraculous origin of Christianity and the fifth to "Modern Negation of Miracles." He devotes a short space to describing that negation and says those united thereon are so:

Because with the truth of miracles the entire citadel of Christianity stands or falls. For its beginning is a miracle; its Author is a miracle; its progress depends upon miracles and they will hereafter be its consummation.

A little further along, he says: "The negation of miracles leads to the annihilation, not merely of the Christian faith, but of all religion. Upon these postulates the learned theologian bases a long argument that is not within the purview of this work, but he quotes Beyschlag, a contemporary, to the effect that one who denies miracles beseeches God in vain for the recovery of a loved child whom He would have healed of illness, and more to the same effect. Dr. Christlieb gives several definitions of miracles, one of which is: Supernatural phenomena, between which and miracles for affirmation of faith, many other orthodox authorities try to draw sharp distinctions.

In tracing the negation of miracles he says their possibility has been doubted for the past 200 years. This seems to imply that belief in them was the rule before in earlier times. He then reviews the positions of the English and German schools of denial, the fears of some churchmen that they foster superstition and asks his hearers to compare Gospel miracles with those of the "Romish and Oriental" churches. On pages 305-7 appear these very positive declarations:

> And do not a multitude of analogies go to show that God can interfere supernaturally at any time in all natural existence?
>
> The man who endeavors to make the laws of nature a ground of proof against miracles, simply begs the question, for he always presupposes what he desires to prove.

Regarding apostolic miracles later than the second century Christlieb cites Tertullian, Origen and Theodore of Mopsueste as witnesses of their performance as late as the year 429. Theodore is thus quoted:

> Many heathen among us have been healed * * * so abundant are miracles in our midst.

After relating the miracles wrought by Hans Egede in Greenland and others mentioned in that connection elsewhere in this work, Christlieb adds the escape of the missionary ship Harmony off the coast of Labrador. An iceberg bore down upon the vessel which was unable to avoid it but when within one foot of the ship and when it seemed inevitable that it must be crushed by the mountain of ice and all on board lost, the iceberg suddenly stopped and then drifted away. He also refers to Luther healing Melancthon and gives an account of the restoration of a girl who had been paralyzed twenty years in South Germany, but is not specific enough to make the case valuable except to say that the healing was publicly certified as a miracle. Toward the close of the chapter occur these significant passages:

> Most of us are aware that wonderful things are related of the healing of the sick in the present day. Yet these are but weak analogies of that divine power of healing in the New Testament history.

In a note on page 335 Spurgeon, the great preacher, is quoted as calling certain German preachers "modern workers of miracles." To his own question regarding miracles: "Do they still occur,'" Dr. Christlieb devotes nine pages of his work. The answer is affirmative and he closes the chapter with the words: "With God nothing shall be impossible."

MARVELOUS VISIONS.

A HARVARD PROFESSOR RELATES MANY ASTONISHING CASES OF SUPERNATURAL SIGHT.

Dr. Edward Hammond Clarke, a physician of Boston who, according to Oliver Wendell Holmes, the poet physician, was at the head of his profession for many years, was the author of a work of 315 pages devoted to visions. The introduction was written by Dr. Holmes, who endorses three of the marvelous cases as those of which he had some personal knowledge. The "essay," as Holmes calls it, was written while Dr. Clarke believed himself to be slowly dying of an internal consuming disease, for which his profession afforded no remedy. His death in 1877 confirmed the belief, and his book was published the following year.

Dr. Holmes says Clarke originally intended to follow his father's profession—the ministry—and it is evident from what is said of him and his parents that Dr. Clarke was "orthodox" as that term is understood in New England. The miraculous character of some of the instances related in the work may therefore be construed as orthodox endorsement of an active belief in the miraculous of the present. In the initiatory chapter of his work, Dr. Clarke treats of the many and various phases and varieties of visions and of the persons who relate them from those whom the Christian world recognizes as

MARVELOUS VISIONS.

prophets, down to the delirium tremens patients. After moralizing on the incredulity of people generally and the indifference of many to the marvelous, he says:

> The persistence with which the truthfulness of the visions has been affirmed, at all times, everywhere, and by such a variety of individuals, is of itself a significant fact, and one that deserves consideration. It implies that below the nonsense, charlatanism, fanaticism, ignorance and mystery, upon which visions are largely built up, there is somewhere a substratum of truth, if we could only get at it. Such a growth could never have appeared, nor would it continue to appear, if its roots did not draw their nutriment from something more invigorating than fancy or deception. It must be admitted, moreover, that the question of the possible occurrence of visions is one of great interest and importance. Its interest lies in its intimate connection with the attractive and a shadowy territory—the terra incognita and debatable ground—which stretches between the body and mind, and which connects this world with the next. Its importance lies in the fact that its solution, if a solution is possible, would not only throw light upon some of the intricate and vexed problems of psychology, but would aid materially in dissipating many popular superstitions and widely spread delusions.

To show how high Dr. Clarke stood as authority in medical science, it is only necessary to cite from an obituary article in the Boston Daily Advertiser, reproduced in Dr. Holmes' introduction. That article says he graduated at Harvard in 1841, got his medical degree in Philadelphia in 1846; was in 1855 chosen professor of materia medica in Harvard University, and resigned in 1872.

Dr. Clarke relates a number of instances in which highly credible persons had visions. Some of these were his own patients and the others were vouched for to him by his professional brethren in whom he could confide. Reviewing the subject of vision after relating seven cases, the author treats of the machinery of normal seeing and hearing, and says:

> If the modicum of truth hidden by the ignorance, superstition and charlatanism which surround such occurrences, could be disinterred from its environment, a real service would be rendered to humanity. For where truth and error are united, if the truth can be discovered, error can be safely left to itself. Nothing dies so quickly as error and falsehood, when there is no truth to animate them.

He then says it is a common but erroneous notion that we see with our eyes and hear with our ears and he proceeds to show that the seat of sensation is the brain. To this he devotes several pages, in the course of which he employs the experiments of Dr. David Ferrier to show that a frog or a pigeon deprived of its brain retains sensation, but has no power of spontaneous action. From these experiments Dr. Clarke concludes that the brain is only one seat of sensation and that there is spinal as well as cerebral consciousness. Notwith-

MARVELOUS VISIONS.

standing the frog and the pigeon, are shown to retain their sight and hearing after the removal of the brain hemispheres, Dr. Clarke fails to show that the brain is not the seat of sensation by which the senses of seeing and hearing are enjoyed.

Dr. Clarke's work is replete with interesting matter, but only a small amount will be cited here in addition to what has been taken. He mentions the case of a young woman who had lost her voice in consequence of a severe attack of bronchitis. He does not say what medical relief was sought, but she asked and obtained the consent of Dr. Ware of Boston to seek aid from "a notorious charlatan, who cured disease in the old ecclesiastical way, by laying of hands on the affected region." This charlatan restored her voice and she was "nettled" because Dr. Ware seemed pleased but not surprised at her recovery. After a year she had another attack and "again put herself under the care of Dr. Ware," from which it appears plain that the doctor failed to cure her before she resorted to the charlatan. Again he failed and again she resorted to the charlatan who failed also. Here it is well to explain that after she was restored the previous year, Dr. Ware gave her his theory of the charlatanry by which she recovered her voice. In consequence, Dr. Ware told her, she had lost faith in the charlatan. Dr. Ware then adopted charlatanry himself; told her to sit down, concentrate all her power of will in an effort to speak and her voice would return. She did as directed and the experiment was so successful that she retained her voice up to the time Dr. Ware told the author of the case.

Dr. Clark on page 277 describes a death-bed scene in which

the patient, a woman of refinement and education, appeared to have a vision and as she expired he says he experienced a sensation that made him perceive that something had departed from her. He does not say he saw anything but Dr. Holmes in his introduction intimates that Dr. Clarke used much more distinct language when relating to him what he experienced. From what both say the inference seems unavoidable that Dr. Clarke had a vision in which he saw the flight of that which is variously termed the soul, spirit, ego or identity, that animates mankind.

As to Dr. Clarke's opinion of visions as realities, the opinion quoted by Dr. Holmes in his introduction is the best index. That opinion is thus expressed:

> Probably all such visions as these are automatic. But yet who, believing in God and personal immortality, as the writer rejoices in doing, will dare to say absolutely all; will dare to assert there is no possible exception.

PROFESSOR FINNEY.

THE GREAT REVIVALIST'S AND EDUCATOR'S CALL AND CAREER MIRACULOUS.

Charles Grandison Finney was one of the most noted, as he was the most scholarly of revivalists of the early and middle part of the nineteenth century. In early life he was religiously inclined and was a prodigy of learning, for which reason his preceptor, when he was about twenty years old, advised him not to go to college, as he could master the Yale course in two years by pursuing his studies in private. Finney adopted the advice and took to teaching. At the age of 24 he began the study of law, was speedily admitted to practice in Adams, Henderson county, New York, and continued in that profession four years. During all this time he was not a Christian in the accepted orthodox sense, though he appears to have been too regular in his attendance at church for the peace of the pastor and of the church-goers whom he worried by his criticisms until that good man declared his presence and leadership of the choir was dangerous to religion.

Until he was 29 years old he had never owned a Bible, but when studying law met so many references to it that he bought one and studied it diligently. During Finney's childhood and youth that part of Northwestern New York in which he was reared was the "far West." Churches and schools were few and poor; preachers were generally ignorant in addition to their rarity and poverty and Finney heard but little preaching that was endurable to him until he went to Connecticut in his twentieth year to pursue an academic course under a Yale graduate. With his mental acuteness and critical disposition he found little satisfaction from the average sermon even in Connecticut and when he went to New Jersey and the South to teach, he heard no more preaching until he settled near his parents' home in Adams, N. Y.

His biographer, G. Frederick Wright, D. D., LL. D., a professor in Oberlin seminary, of which institution Prof. Finney was for many years president, who tells the story of his conversion, compares it to that of Saul of Tarsus. He says: "In Finney's own opinion this version of Gospel truth was in a large degree the result of the direct operation of the Holy Spirit upon his mind." And he continues:

> The main facts of the Gospel, though in unattractive form, had, without doubt, been brought within his survey by the faithful pastors in Warren and in Adams, and perhaps even by those unlettered itinerants to whom he had listened in earlier days; while his own resistance to the manifold claims of duty had wrought up to the highest degree within him that sense of the need of divine grace which is the starting point of all true religious faith. Upon these elements of truth the illuminating spirit now descended as in a lightning stroke, and helped him to see the broad and reasonable basis upon which the Christian rests his hope of life and immortality.

PROFESSOR FINNEY.

In the busy street and in the light of day, there came to him a vision of Christ, transfixing him to the spot where he stood and arresting his whole train of worldly thought. For a considerable time he stood motionless where the vision met him, until at last he yielded to the summons and resolved that he would accept Christ that day or die in the attempt.

In pursuance of this resolution, Finney retired to a deep wood and passed many hours in great perturbation of mind, which closed with a deep and earnest prayer for grace and more light. In the evening while alone in his office he again resorted to prayer and, as his biographer says, "he seemed to have a vision of the Lord and that Christ met him face to face." This vision his biographer calls an illusion in which he seemed to see Christ as a man. On being aroused he sat down by his fire and "received what he describes as 'a mighty baptism of the Holy Ghost.' This was an experience he was not looking for and of which he did not remember to have heard before." It is thus described:

> It seemed to him as if there was a positive force like electricity entering and penetrating his whole system. He wept aloud with joy and love and, to use his own words, 'literally bellowed out the unutterable gushings of his heart.'

What followed his conversion was almost as miraculous as that event itself. In the morning Finney received a second "baptism of the Holy Ghost" and he resolved to at once respond to what he regarded as the Lord's call upon him to preach.

When a deacon of the church reminded him that he was to appear for him in a suit to be tried that morning, he told the litigant that he had been retained by the Lord Jesus and could not try the case. The deacon thereupon settled his suit and betook himself to prayer. The noise of Finney's conversion, circulated largely by himself, caused an impromptu meeting that evening and Finney made an open profession of religion, whereupon the minister, Mr. Gale, confessed that he had expressed a doubt of God's power to convert such a sinner as Finney had been. Thenceforth Finney devoted himself largely to revival work and many who are still living as the nineteenth century is closing will remember to have heard him in what is now the central West. His career as a revivalist, especially his earliest years, were full of events that partook of the miraculous. Among these occurrences were several visitations like that which brought about his conversion. During the third year of his work as a revivalist and the first year after his ordination, those physical manifestations known among the vulgar as "the jerks" made their appearance among his audiences and put an end to a violent controversy between Presbyterians, who had been exempt thitherto, and the Baptists, who had experienced them before Finney's arrival.

The work from which this sketch has been derived was published in 1891 and it quotes from Dr. Aiken's Historical Sketch of Presbyterianism, thus: "After forty years, I am persuaded that it (Finney's revival work) was the work of God."

Finney's belief in miracles was not confined to his early

experiences. It did not cease with his conversion or his career as a revivalist. When he became a settled pastor in New York city, he says he found that he knew "comparatively little about Christ and that a multitude of things were said about Him in the Gospel of which I had no spiritual view, and of which I knew little or nothing." How he learned more may best be told in his own words, viz.:

> What I did know of Christ was almost exclusively as an atoning and justifying Savior. But as a Jesus to save men from sin, or as a sanctifying Savior, I knew very little about him. This was made, by the spirit of God, very clear to my mind. And it deeply convinced me that I must know more of the Gospel in my own experience, and have more of Christ in my heart, or I never could expect to benefit the church. In that state of mind, I used often to tell the Lord Jesus Christ that I was sensible I knew very little about Him, and I besought Him to reveal Himself to me, that I might be instrumental in revealing Him to others. I used especially to pray over particular passages and classes of passages in the Gospel, that speak of Christ, that I might apprehend their meaning and feel their power in my own heart. And I was often strongly convinced that I desired this for the purpose of making Christ known to others.
>
> I will not enter into details with regard to the way Christ led me. Suffice it to say, and alone to the honor of His grace do I say it, that He has taught me

some things that I asked him to show me. Since my own mind became impressed in the manner in which I have spoken, I have felt as strongly and unequivocally pressed by the spirit of God to labor for the sanctification of the church as I once did for the conversion of sinners.

It will be apparent from this that Prof. Finney believed in the inspiration of modern evangelists. This belief must have been greatly strengthened by letters and from other sources that God rewarded his later labors by "awakening a spirit of inquiry on the subject of holiness throughout the church, both in this country and in Europe."

His views were opposed by the leading New School Calvinists, who took measures to avoid responsibility for him and to preach against the new doctrine which he promulgated as a result of this inspiration, which he called "sanctification."

As Finney never retracted but continued to prosper and grow in popularity, it seems evident that the opposition gave to his belief the approval of silence, so far as the New School Presbyterians were concerned.

Finney disagreed with the Presbyterians in the matter of church government while in New York, and his church withdrew from that connection and became Congregational long before he devoted himself to Oberlin college. His belief in miracles and the endorsement of his belief of his miraculous calling and inspiration by Presbyterians and Congregationalists for half a century should of itself estop both from pleading that the age of miracles is past.

PROFESSOR FINNEY.

The history of Oberlin college, as given in the biography of Finney by G. F. Wright, a professor in that institution, shows that the first president of the then "Oberlin academy" was miraculously or divinely guided to secure Finney. President Shepherd had started for Cincinnati on hearing that Lane seminary was being rent asunder by the negro question, to secure talent for his school. The roads were so execrable that he had decided to go to New York instead, because he could travel on the old national road while travel on the mud roads, 150 miles, to Cincinnati seemed impossible.

At a tavern where he sojourned to rest his horses and himself after a tedious pull to a central Ohio point, he met Theodore Keep, son of one of the directors of Oberlin, who urged him to proceed to Cincinnati and secure Asa Mahan, who was about to retire from the presidency of Lane. Keep also urged him to then continue his journey to New York and secure Finney, who had then reached almost the height of his fame as an evangelist.*

Finney encountered not only stout opposition from Congregational and Presbyterian ministers, but from others also. Some of this opposition reached the point of violence, much of it because he made several innovations upon what were considered established and respectable methods of revival work. Principal among his innovations was the "anxious seat," or "mourners' bench," of which his biographer says he was the inventor.

---

* Biography of Finney by Wright, pp. 125 to 135

Among those who were stoutest in their opposition was Lyman Beecher, the patriarch of the talented tribe of preachers. Beecher told Finney to his face that if he ever entered New England he would meet him at the boundary and contest every inch of ground with him. At that time, Finney was a Presbyterian. After some years, when a daughter of Beecher asked Finney if he were not going to visit Boston, he answered: "Not until your father invites me." Within a short time the orthodox ministers of Boston united in an invitation or request that Finney visit that city "and lo! the name of Lyman Beecher led the rest."

In describing the work Finney did in the New England metropolis, Dr. Edward Beecher, son of the man who had declared war on him, said he honored Finney "and loved him as one as truly commissioned by God to declare His will as were Isaiah, Jeremiah, Ezekiel or Paul."

The conversion of Lyman Beecher from a violent opponent to a friend, Finney regarded as one of the many evidences he had received of God's special interposition to prosper his work.

WILLIAMS COLLEGE.

PRESIDENT MARK HOPKINS BELIEVES THAT MIRACLES COME IN ANSWER TO PRAYER.

Mark Hopkins, D. D., LL. D., for many years president of Williams college, in his "Law of Love and Love as Law," has a chapter devoted to prayer. In this he says prayer is not simply desire but paramount desire and that any form of asking for anything, except for that for which this desire is paramount, would not be asking. He says, p. 302, that any other asking would be hypocrisy to the omniscient eye and continues:

> It is only a paramount desire presented to God with the submission becoming a creature, that is prayer, and the question is whether, in consequence of such prayer man would receive what he would not without it. On this point the Bible raises no doubt. There is in that no recognition of the difficulties raised by philosophy.

In the matter of praying for rain Dr. Hopkins quotes approvingly from the Duke of Argyle's "Reign of Law," thus:

> There are no phenomena visible to man of which it is true to say they are governed by any invariable force. That which does govern them is always some variable combination of invariable forces.

Upon this idea, carried out to its full development, Dr Hopkins reasons:

> If, as some suppose, man can cause rain by the firing of cannon, then it may be obtained by asking it, even of Him. In such a case there would be simply a different adjustment of invariable laws; and if results may be thus produced to some extent by the intervention of human will, without a miracle, it cannot be irrational to suppose they may be thus produced to any extent by divine will.

Answers to Prayer.

THE POWER OF PRAYER.

A PIOUS GERMAN'S COLLECTION OF CASES OF HEALING BY FAITH.

A modest little book published in German in Cincinnati under the title, "Power of the Prayer of Faith," contains between seventy-five and one hundred instances in which prayers were answered in striking ways. The author, Karl Gottlob Schuh, gives no indication of his own standing in any church or in the community in which he lives—Greenville, Ohio—but it is evident that he is a man of great piety and on terms of sufficient familiarity with people prominent in the religious world, to have received their consent to quote them as witnesses.

The first miracle story in this book is attributed to "a well-known man of God." Shorn of its superfluous verbiage, it is this: The narrator, who was pastor of a church, found at his gate at daybreak a member of his congregation, weeping because her husband had gone away saying he would not return until the religious excitement then prevailing should abate. As it was about time for an early morning prayer meeting, he conducted the woman thither and the congregation united in praying for the conversion of the fugitive. At a night meeting the supplications were renewed and with great fervor and solemnity. To the astonishment of the congrega-

THE POWER OF PRAYER. 107

tion the recreant entered, proclaimed his renunciation of Universalism and said that while riding away he was overcome by a sense of his guilt and knew he must be born again. This man, the author relates upon his own account, is now one of the elders of a Presbyterian church and one of the most diligent servants of God that can be found.

The value of this and many accounts of miraculous healings and conversions, is impaired if not destroyed by the failure of the author to properly authenticate them. The same is true to a degree of the story of his own experience in being healed of dyspepsia and catarrh, because he admits that his book was published before the healing was complete. The work is all the author of this work desires, however, because it is proof that orthodox Protestants do not all believe that the age of miracles is past. With what other evidence is here produced and precedes this chapter, it is in the nature of corroborative evidence. For further corroboration Mr. Schuh quotes Dwight L. Moody, J. S. Inskip, Bishop Bowman and others who are less prominent in the Christian world.

The story of Bishop Bowman is of the healing by prayer of Bishop Simpson. Bowman was attending a conference of the Methodist Episcopal Church in Indiana in 1858 when the illness of Bishop Simpson was announced and Bishop Jones, who presided, asked the conference to unite in prayer for his restoration. William Taylor, the eminent missionary (since a bishop), led, and Bowman says he never heard so powerful a prayer. While on his knees he was impressed that the bishop would recover and he made a note of the exact time of this manifestation. When next he saw the bishop that prelate was at work as ably and diligently as ever. Bowman asked the bishop concerning his recovery and learned that the turning point of his disease was at the exact moment when he, Bowman, experienced the sensation described above, and during the prayer in the conference. The doctors had given him up and left his room. When they returned an hour later they were astounded at the improvement that had taken place during their absence, contrary to all human experience and expectation.

Inskip's story in brief is that illness had hindered him in his evangelistic work and threatened to end it and his earthly career. He describes his affliction in full in a letter dated May 27, 1879. Though an evangelist, he seems not to have thought of resorting to prayer until suddenly attacked in Boston by a headache that compelled him to relinquish the conduct of an afternoon meeting. His hostess advised him to seek relief in prayer and quoted to him James v-14, 15. He and his host's family followed the suggestion; he was healed; conducted the evening meeting and had no return of his malady.

One case, the authority for which is given as Dr. Edwin F. Hatfield, a well-known preacher of the Presbyterian Church, in the State of New York; is that of a little girl who was healed of paralysis and a serious affection of the hip-joint, both resulting from accident. After a season at a hospital and medical and surgical treatment, without avail, the child of 9 or 10 years was taken home and the pious mother resorted to prayer. Weeks of almost unremitting supplication, pious conversation

THE POWER OF PRAYER.

and study of the accounts of healings by the Lord Jesus when on earth followed. One day while thus engaged the little girl rose to get a drink of water when she suddenly called out: "Mother! See, I can walk again!" From that moment the girl found her crutches superfluous and examination showed that a great ulcer, which was among her afflictions, had disappeared; the dislocation of the hip was reduced and the afflicted leg had been restored to as great perfection as the other. The girl was 21 years old when her mother related the case to Dr. Hatfield and had had no return of the maladies, but had been healed of another dangerous illness fifteen months after her first healing.

Mr. Schuh publishes from Miss Carrie F. Judd of Buffalo, N. Y., who had considerable reputation as a faith-healer, the account of her healing. As her case may not be regarded as one proper to classify among evangelical Protestant cases, I will only say concerning it that its incorporation in Mr. Schuh's book gives it at least a partial standing in that class.

The most remarkable case related by Mr. Schuh is that of Miss Jennie Smith of Dayton, Ohio, once of Middleburg or Spring Hills, Champaign county, of the same State. Through a series of misfortunes Miss Smith lost health; powers of locomotion and paternal protection, all within a short time. Beside this, her father before his death had lost all his property and left his widow and nine children in poverty. Miss Smith traveled constantly as a missionary in a wheeled couch and after suffering and working sixteen years, without receiving any relief from doctors, she went to Philadelphia for treatment in 1378. Her physician being a Christian, she suggested to him that prayer be tried instead of a surgical operation and he consented. Three ministers who had been stationed in Dayton while Miss Smith lived there happened to be residing in Philadelphia and were present at her request when the prayer was offered. When faith had almost fled and strength forsaken her, she recalled the story of the withered hand. It seemed as if the heavens opened and an electric stream swept through her entire system and gave it new strength. She raised herself to a sitting position; her physician sprang to her side and let down the footboard of her wheel-chair, she sprang out, ran around the room and sang: "Praise God From All Blessings Flow." Miss Smith, says the author, now works great blessings among the railroad men in Eastern cities and goes about on foot instead of being wheeled in a chair as formerly.

Moody's story, located in Scotland, is much like that of the miraculous conversion of the Universalist attributed to an unnamed pastor, in the first story herein referred to, and is no better authenticated. Nearly all of the other stories in this work depend upon the credulity of the reader to believe the words of unknown men and in many cases of men to whom the author gives neither habitation nor name.

AN EXALTED AUTHORITY.

QUEEN VICTORIA'S CHAPLAIN ON ANSWERS TO PRAYER BY MIRACULOUS MEANS.

A very ordinary looking book bearing the title: "The New Cyclopaedia of Illustrative Anecdote" is the product of the genius of Rev. Donald Macleod, D. D., Chaplain to Her Majesty, and editor of "Good Words." Anecdote 288, illustrative of the efficacy of prayer, tells how Rev. Richard Cecil was delivered from the hands of three robbers on East Grinstead Common. The minister when surrounded thought it "an occasion for faith" and recalled the Scripture passage: "Call upon me in time of trouble and I will deliver thee." When the leader asked him who he was, etc., and learned his identity, he ordered the others to let him go. As Mr. Cecil had £16 on his person, he felt the escape to be miraculous, though the robber assured him he was released because the leader had heard him preach and knew him.

Anecdote 856 tells of a lady traveling in her own coach, finding it hampered with provisions, ordered her servant to give the food away. The governess obtained leave to be the almoner and sought out the neatest premises in the village. There she found a starving woman on her knees praying for food and gave her a hamper full of choice viands. The poor woman, without rising, thanked God for having sent her the food. The writer of the story does not say in what country or at what date this occurred, but it is to be inferred that it was in the Christian land of Great Britain.

Anecdote 872 is of Heine, Berlin's famous physician, who lost all his savings by a bank failure. The loss almost deprived him of reason, but he resorted to prayer and his cheerfulness and hope were restored.

Number 874 is so striking that I am almost tempted to copy it entire. It tells of a party of Moravian ministers on the Britania, from London to St. Thomas, in the West Indies, when the ship was attacked by pirates. The missionaries retired to the cabin to pray when the crew prepared for battle. The pirate fired several broadsides and, though within grappling distance, failed to hit the Britania. The pirates threw grapplers, but failed to catch them and when they thought they could destroy the mission ship by more firing, a sudden squall prevented their shots taking effect. When the smoke of battle rose the pirate saw the Britania sailing serenely away under full canvass. On this the compiler comments: "Thus wonderfully did God answer prayer and save the vessel."

These few, taken from among many similar anecdotes, should be sufficient to show that the chaplain to Queen Victoria of England, etc., believed in miracles as late as 1872, when the Rev. Dr. Thomas Guthrie of Edinburgh wrote to Dr. Macleod a letter commending his work which the compiler says was intended as an aid to the teacher and preacher in the school or the pulpit. Dr. Guthrie says it must be of great service to the ministry "by furnishing them with suitable and striking illustrations of both its doctrines and its duties."

One incident I cannot forbear to mention, though it is foreign to the object of this work. It tells of Archbishop Usher, having heard much of Rev. Samuel Rutherford's piety, decided to visit him when visiting Scotland. Disguised as a pauper he begged lodging of the famous preacher, who seated him in the kitchen while he apprised Mrs. Rutherford of his presence.

Mrs. R., desirous of testing the orthodoxy of her guest, asked him how many commandments there were and he answered: "Eleven." The pious woman rebuked his ignorance sharply and sent him to bed in a garret. Mr. Rutherford, hearing him at prayer, decided to treat him more becomingly and, having learned his identity, invited him to occupy his pulpit. The archbishop accepted and took for his text: "A new commandment give I unto you," etc.

Mrs. Rutherford was deeply humiliated, of course, when she learned that she had snubbed an archbishop while entertaining an angel unawares. This same story is told and in much more interesting form in Dr. J. V. Watson's book, which is mentioned in the chapter devoted to Methodists. Its author was no less notable writer than T. S. Arthur, who was famed in his days as a writer of highly moral fiction.

TO HELP PREACHERS.

A BOOK WITH MIRACLE STORIES TO ENLIVEN AND ILLUSTRATE SERMONS.

Miracles seem to play an important part in the instruction of ministers. In books published for their benefit and to aid them in preaching, special providences and answers to prayer form the bases of many anecdotes compiled to enable preachers to liven their sermons and illustrate points therein. One of these books is "The Dictionary of Anecdote and Illustrative Fact," compiled by Rev. Walter Baxendale, author of "The Preacher's Commentary on the Book of Ruth." The author's name is not important, as he gives his authority for most of the anecdotes, some of whom are eminent in the religious world. These stories are attributed to Spurgeon. The second is put in condensed form to save room:

SPURGEON ON PRAYER.

A preacher, whose sermons had converted men by scores, received a revelation from heaven that not one of the conversions was owing to his talents or eloquence, but all to the prayers of an illiterate lay-brother who sat on the pulpit steps, pleading all the time for the success of the sermon.

Some two years ago a poor woman came to my vestry in deep distress because her husband had ab-

TO HELP PREACHERS.   115

sconded. When her tale was told I said: "All we could do was to kneel and cry to the Lord for the conversion of your husband." We knelt and prayed and when we rose I bade the woman not to fret as I felt sure the deserter would return. Some months later, when I had forgotten the incident, the woman came, accompanied by her husband, who had been converted. Inquiry showed that on the very day we prayed for him; while he was at sea, he found a stray copy of one of my sermons, read it, and was converted. As soon as possible, he returned to his wife and was admitted to the church.

I sat side by side with a brother minister not many days ago, who remarked to me: "I'm afraid many of our people do not believe in prayer." "Oh, dear!" I said, "I would not be a minister of such a church five minutes."

An extract from an interview with Spurgeon, taken from the Pall Mall Gazette is to the effect that his faith in the efficacy of prayer was growing stronger and firmer than ever.

It is not a matter of faith with me, but of knowledge and everyday experience. I am constantly witnessing the most unmistakable answers to prayer. * * * Look at my orphanage. To keep it going entails an annual expenditure of about £10,000. Only £1400 is provided by endowment. The remaining £8000 comes to me regularly in answer to prayer. I do not know where I shall get it from day to day. I ask God for it and He sends it.

LUTHER'S BELIEF.

Martin Luther is often quoted by those religionists who discountenance belief in miracles, but the compiler of this dictionary has found several extracts from his sayings in support of a belief in the miraculous answer to prayer. Tholuck is quoted to the effect that at the time the diet of Nuremberg was held, Luther was praying at home. At the very hour when the edict granting free toleration to Protestants was granted he ran out of his house crying out: "We have gained the victory!"

Anecdote 4253 tells of Luther's prayers prolonging Melancthon's life. Melancthon was supposed to be on his deathbed when Luther hastened to him and aroused him by a sorrowful exclamation, when Melancthon begged to be allowed to depart in peace. Luther replied: "We can't spare you yet," fell upon his knees and prayed fervently for his recovery. He then ordered some soup and bade Melancthon eat it. When he declined Luther threatened to excommunicate him. Melancthon obeyed and recovered. When Luther returned home he told his wife: "God gave me my brother Melancthon back, in direct answer to my prayers." Luther is also thus quoted:

> Just as a shoemaker makes a shoe or a tailor a coat, so also ought the Christian to pray. The Christian's trade is praying, and the prayer of the church works great miracles. In our day it has raised from the dead three persons, viz.: myself, having been fre-

quently sick unto death; my wife, Catharine, who likewise was dangerously ill, and Melancthon, who was sick unto death at Weimar. And though their rescue from sickness and other bodily dangers be but trifling miracles, nevertheless they must be exhibited for the sake of those whose faith is weak.

OTHER AUTHORITIES.

The Christian Age, a religious paper, is credited with anecdote 4249. It tells of a pastor who devoted a week to studying a sermon, which suddenly, on Saturday, "became to him stale and dry" and "instantly another text lodged into his mind" and rapidly ran into a sermon which he preached Sunday morning. At the close of the service a lady remained "to confer with the session of the church respecting a profession of faith." She belonged to a Catholic family, but the light received from that sermon had converted her. In accounting for the change of sermon, the writer in the Age says a friend of the lady had been praying eleven years for her conversion and that on the Saturday when the minister made the change a party of the lady's friends had "united in praying that the pastor might on the next Sabbath say something that would meet the case of the lady who was expected to be present in the church on that morning."

C. T. Harris is authority for the story that a pious lady in Hereford, England, while praying became impressed that she ought to send £50 to a Mr. Bourne "for carrying on the work of the Lord." After conferring with her mother, she decided to test the correctness of her impression. Her brother was dispatched to Bemersley to investigate. In an interview with Mr. Bourne he asked that gentleman if he had been praying for "anything special." Mr. B. promptly responded: "Yes, for £50; for we are in great need of that sum," which was given him. Mr. Harris seems to have been so deeply impressed with this miracle that he forgot to say in what branch of the Lord's work Mr. Bourne was engaged. He seems to have considered Mr. Bourne and his work to be too well known to have needed description or explanation.

Krummacher, a somewhat celebrated German writer on religious subjects, is the author of a story of healing through the prayer of a four-year-old child. The child's mother was so ill that the doctors had given her up. When the child heard the verdict "she went into an adjoining room, knelt down and said: 'Dear Lord Jesus, oh make mother well again.' After she had thus prayed she said, as though in God's name, 'Yes, my dear child, I will do it gladly.'" The child then ran to her mother and assured her she would get well, which she did. Upon this incident, which is here greatly abbreviated Krummacher comments thus:

> Is it, then, always permitted for me to pray thus unconditionally respecting temporal concerns? No, thou must not venture to do so, if whilst you ask you doubt.

From Stephenson's "Praying and Working" is quoted a remark of one who stood by the grave of Gossner and the editor says it was not hyperbole, viz.:

> He prayed up the walls of an hospital and the hearts of the nurses; he prayed missionary stations

into being and missionaries into faith; he prayed open the hearts of the rich and gold from the most distant lands.

Dr. Liefchild is given as authority for a case in which a Christian traveling in Italy heard of a young soldier who was condemned to be shot at 9 o'clock of the morning he heard of it while he was at breakfast. He at once retired to pray for the soldier's salvation; that, if he were not prepared to die, his execution might be postponed until he should repent. While on his knees the Christian heard a volley and was soon obliged to hasten from the town. About two months later he read in a paper that, though that volley was fired at the condemned soldier, not a bullet took effect. So miraculous was the escape considered that his pardon was granted.

Archdeacon Farrar is given as authority for this: "More than one saint, like St. Francis, and like Wesley, has left behind the record that God has never refused him anything for which he seriously prayed. It can gain for us everything, not perhaps, that we wish, but everything that we want."

At least half a score of other cases of answers to prayer are given in this book, but they are not authenticated. They include rescue of vessels from destruction; escape from death in battle, from sharks, the raising of wind to turn mills when people were suffering for bread; the capture of a negro and his wife as slaves that they might be converted.

That these anecdotes have been employed by preachers is evinced by the fact that the volume I have used has been well thumbed and has many little crosses marked against paragraphs, some of which are here mentioned. Though I have not cited all of the cases which appear miraculous, it is a little remarkable that only two paragraphs about miracles are noted in the index. One of these stories is attributed to Luther as exposing a fraud and the other is a remark of an Oxford professor, viz.: "If you believe in miracles you will be nothing better and if you do not, you will be nothing worse."

Anecdote 4961 is attributed to The Hague Tageblatti. (Newspaper, date not given.) It tells of an infidel paper manufacturer who said he would have machinery work Sundays and weekdays alike and make more money. The inauguration of the machinery was celebrated by a feast in the works, during which the paper maker scoffingly compared his boilers to hell. Almost at that moment the boilers exploded and killed the scoffer.

This naturally recalls the sensational story that appears semi-periodically in American newspapers of the man who is stricken dumb, blind or deaf for blasphemous revilings when excessive rain, drouth or other untoward conditions have ruined his crops or otherwise sent accumulated misfortunes upon him. These stories are nearly always so located that verification or refutation is difficult, but the eagerness with which they are utilized by many ministers in their exhortations is abundant evidence that there is a very widespread belief in so much of the miraculous as suits the purposes or prejudices of those who hear marvelous stories like these.

CALIFORNIA MIRACLES.

A PREACHER MYSTERIOUSLY SUPPLIED WITH MEANS TO DEFEAT AN INFIDEL.

Rev. W. H. Briggs is a minister of the Christian church who, as this article is being written, is being written about and read about as the minister who turned street railroad conductor to make a living rather than whine to be taken back into the church after the hand of fellowship had been withdrawn. Mr. Briggs is an A. M., and has lived in San Joaquin county, California, since childhood and during most of his manhood has been a preacher of the Christian Church, which is generally known as the Campbellite.

In 1883 he was challenged to discuss with Colonel Kelso, a well-known resident of that county and equally well known as a champion of Colonel Robert G. Ingersoll's views of religion. Briggs accepted without hesitation, but felt hardly equal to the contest as Col. Kelso was regarded as the "boss agnostic" of that region. The debates were to be held at two points in the county, one of which was generally regarded as infidel headquarters.

Briggs was not as well equipped for the debate as he desired to be. He had never read more than fragments of Ingersoll's lectures, which he assumed would form the basis of Col. Kelso's speeches. He found it impossible to send away for a copy of any of his lectures and prayed earnestly that the Lord would furnish him the information by some means. He also prayed for a copy of the works of Wilford Hall, a noted Universalist writer. The time was growing short for answers to his prayers when, as he was driving from Clements to Brand House one dusty day, his horse shied at something in the road and as he passed the object he saw it was a book. He reined in his horse and found the book not six inches from the track of the buggy wheels. It was brand new and on examination he found it to be a volume of Ingersoll's lectures. Who lost it he never could discover and it remained long in his library.

The next Sunday he held services at Woodbridge, when a young lady, who is now the wife of a public officer of San Joaquin county, met him just before the services opened and handed him a copy of Dr. Hall's work, saying her father thought it would be of use to him in the forthcoming debate. He had not expressed his wish for either of these works to any mortal and had no opportunity of communicating them to anyone in Woodbridge.

Mr. Briggs' heart was greatly lightened. He read both works and if the testimony of those who heard the eight days' debate is conclusive evidence, the Lord enabled him to defeat his agnostic adversary. The Lord's intervention did not end with the furnishing of the ammunition for the debate. It resulted in the building of churches at Acampo and Elliott, in San Joaquin county, the latter place having been regarded as a field in which it would be idle to hope for a church. Very naturally, Mr. Briggs and his friends, who are numerous throughout San Joaquin and neighboring counties, think the Lord wrought at least three miracles in connection with that debate.

NON-RELIGIOUS MIRACLES.

MARVELOUS WORKS WHEREIN PRAYER OR FAITH HAD NO PART.

It seems astonishing that many people who doubt that even Jesus of Nazareth performed the miracles attributed to him in the Gospels are very ready to believe accounts of healings quite as marvelous when performed by men who make no pretension to being reformers or even to religious belief.

Who does not remember or has not heard of Dr. Newton, who, a generation ago, traveled all over the United States and perhaps Europe also, performing instantaneous cures of many forms of disease and "coining" money thereby. He was not attacked by the pulpit or the press because he did not try to organize a new sect, and he did pay well for advertising.

A quarter of a century later a "Boy Wonder" made tours of the whole country on a like mission. He was widely advertised and paid handsomely for daily "write-ups" in the daily newspapers. That he performed astonishing cures there are witnesses in nearly every town and city he visited. He was a boy when he set out in his career, but must be nearly thirty-five years old now. After he visited the Pacific coast about 1894, he decided to remain in the East and the company of which he was the star found another boy wonder and, without a change in their dead-wall, show-paper or advertising, they made another tour.

PROTESTANT MIRACLES.

While in Stockton, California, they heard of B. M. Hohenshell, a former farmer, who discovered in young manhood that he possessed great magnetic powers which he utilized for healing the sick, but Mr. Hohenshell declined a tempting offer to become a boy wonder abroad. He continued his practice at home, does not advertise but goes about his work much as does a physician, doing all the good he can in a modest way, making plenty of money probably, but doing a vast amount of work without hope of pecuniary reward. He believes in his power and uses it to the best of his ability. I have no words except those of commendation for him though I do not know him personally. I have within a few years heard much of his almost angelic ministrations and honor him for the good he has done. I do think it strange—passing strange, however, that those who firmly believe in "Barney" Hohenshell's power should disbelieve the evidence of their own eyes and ears in the form of friends and acquaintances who have been restored to health by the aid of Christian Science after the doctors had given them up. Beside these there are all around Mr. Hohenshell's home many who were given up to die by the drug-doctors within from one to three months and who turned to science and have survived, now, from a few months to several years.

Some years ago the London Medical Times contained an account of an experiment on four condemned men in Russia. They were put to sleep on beds whereon victims of cholera had died, but were ignorant of the fact. After ample time being given for the dread disease to develop not one gave any symptom of the plague. They were subsequently told that they must sleep on beds that had been occupied by cholera patients and, though the beds were perfectly clean and had not been so occupied, three of them were attacked by cholera and died within four hours.

MIRACLE OF THE MULE.

One of the most widely believed notions of the laws of nature is that hybrids are barren. So firmly fixed is this idea that efforts to test its truth are rare, if they are ever made. The idea was crystallized by "Josh Billings," I think, in his reference to a temporary political party. He said it was like a mule because it was without pride of ancestry or hope of posterity. It is a well-established fact, however, that James Journeay of Stockton, California, is the owner of a mule mare that bore a colt. The animal, now (1899) about seven years old, is on Mr. Journeay's ranch, five or six miles from Stockton. When so young that the motherhood of the mule could be demonstrated by her suckling the colt, both mother and foal were publicly exhibited on the plaza or Hunter-street square in Stockton and the fact is susceptible of ample proof.

I do not cite this well-attested fact as evidence that a miracle has occurred during the last decade of the nineteenth century, but to show that not all of nature's laws are understood by present day philosophers. Though Mr. Journeay's mule is not an exceptional animal in any other way, she is such an exception in that one regard as to break the supposed rule or to show that to supposed laws of nature there can be exceptions which by no means prove the rule.

PROTESTANT MIRACLES.

A PHYSICAL MIRACLE.

In a recent number of McClure's Magazine is an article on the new power derived from the liquifaction of air. The accomplishment of this liquefaction would have been pronounced a miracle by most scientists as late as the noon of the present century, if not even as late as the last decade thereof. The article shows that liquified air not only solves the supposed insoluble problem of perpetual motion, but actually multiplies its own power indefinitely and accomplishes many other wonders. The discoverer of the process declares that it will solve the problem of aerial navigation and makes his opinion appear very plausible. This notice of the discovery and its wonders is sufficient for my purpose here, but those who are skeptical concerning present day miracles should read the article which appears in the March number for 1899 of McClure's.

NEWSPAPER MIRACLES.

While religious as well as secular newspapers either discredit or ignore accounts of non-sensational as well as religious miracles, they both employ the adjective "miraculous" to describe narrow or marvelous escapes from death. So common is the habit that they often tell their readers that occurrences are miracles and then proceed to so describe them that every element of the miraculous is eliminated. That this is but a criticism on the language they employ I admit in part, but not in toto and especially as regards the religious press in which it is comparatively common to find stories of answers to prayers and events that are properly classifiable as miracles.

I have recently read a newspaper story of the mysterious

circulation of news in the prison at Dannemora, N. Y. This story says the convicts often know the result of a prize-fight or other "sporting" event before the officers of the prison know it, though every effort is made to keep the news from reaching them. It also says the convicts know when executions are to take place, though they are not allowed to have newspapers containing the news and every means is employed to keep them in ignorance.

This naturally recalls the accounts of missionaries in India who first told the world of the mysterious means by which information was transmitted by natives in that country far in advance of the swiftest means known to the whites. During the Sepoy rebellion in that country, this mysterious power was often mentioned and respectable British authority said the disaster at Cawnpore was known among the native population of the cities in the possession of the British long before the swiftest horses could bear couriers with reports to the officials. One writer, cited I think by Lecky, says the first accounts of the disaster were received from Parsee merchants.

HYMNS THAT BETRAY.

EXTRACTS FROM PETITIONS IN VERSE, FOR SPECIAL FAVORS FROM PROVIDENCE.

If Protestantism has rejected the miraculous it should revise its hymnology to suit its profession. In opening a little volume of Gospel Hymns, published in 1883, the first that arrested my attention was that beautiful poem, "Jesus Lover of My Soul." The third verse is a refutation of the pretense. It reads:

> Thou, O Christ, art all I want;
> More than all in thee I find:
> Raise the fallen, cheer the faint
> Heal the sick and lead the blind.

Hymn No. 90 of the same volume, which is a compilation of the songs used by Evangelist Moody, contains this:

> I leave it all with Jesus,
> For He knows
> How to steal the bitter
> From life's woes;
> How to gild the tear-drop
> With His smile,
> Make the desert garden
> Bloom awhile.

Number 107 of these hymns is a rhyming version of that

HYMNS THAT BETRAY.

sublime poem Psalm xxiii, which promises many earthly blessings and immunities. This may be said to be so strictly poetical as not to constitute a basis for a valid argument, but if it is to be so regarded then Holy Writ must be at least half repudiated while the poem is taught and will probably always be taught in the Sunday schools as one of the greatest of religious gems.

Who that ever read Newman's "Lead, Kindly Light" doubted that it was a prayer for inspiration? After it had been banished from the hymnals of the Anglican church for many years after the author became a Catholic, it has reappeared and can now be found in the books of nearly all denominations.

The hymnal of the Protestant Episcopal church in the United States, of 1874, approved by the general convention of that church in the same year, contains hymns of which the following are extracts:

No. 264—Star of hope, gleam on the billow,
    Bless the soul that sighs for thee,
    Bless the sailor's lonely pillow,
    Far, far at sea.

No. 267—Eternal Father! strong to save,
    Whose arm hath bound the restless wave,
    Who bid'st the mighty ocean deep
    Its own appointed limits keep;
    Oh hear us when we cry to thee
    For those in peril on the sea.

No. 269—To Thee I raised my humble prayer
    To snatch me from the grave;

I found Thine ear not slow to hear
Nor short Thine arm to save.

These are all for help to those who go down to the sea in ships, but there are others that pray for divine inspiration, help, etc. The following are from hymns on the ordination of ministers:

No. 270—Lord, pour Thy Spirit from on high,
And Thine ordained servants bless;
Graces and gifts to each supply,
And clothe Thy priests with righteousness.

No. 271—Clothe then, with energy divine
Their words and let those words be Thine;
To them Thy sacred truth reveal,
Suppress their fear, inflame their zeal.

Verse 3 of hymn 254 reads:

Choose Thou for me my friends,
My sickness or my health;
Choose Thou my cares for me,
My poverty or wealth.
Not mine, not mine the choice,
In things or great or small
Be Thou my guide, my strength,
My wisdom and my all.

Hymn No. 249, under the head of "Visitation of the Sick," bids the patient cast aside fear, assures him that the Lord will provide. The fourth verse reads:

Did ever trouble yet befall,
And He refuse to hear thy call?

HYMNS THAT BETRAY.

And has He not His promise past
That thou shalt overcome at last?

It will strike the student of Christian Science that those who have endorsed this or who adhere to a church of whose service it is a part, are estopped from denouncing prayer cure, faith cure, or any other form of healing in which prayer is even a part.

As the Moody hymns represent all whom the Episcopal people group under the general head of "the sects," I do not care to quote more copiously from their hymns. I have quoted more freely from the Anglican book because it represents a church that has been most conspicuous in past years for its attack upon the miraculous.

In a collection of hymns compiled in 1885 by C. C. Cline and published in Covington, Ky., No. 8 contains this as verse 4:

Comfort those who weep and mourn;
Let the time of joy return;
Those that are cast down lift up;
Make them strong in faith and hope.

No. 62, by Isaac Watts, whose orthodoxy will not be disputed, contains this verse:

He pardons all thy sins,
Prolongs thy feeble breath;
He healeth thine infirmities
And ransoms thee from death.

The "Illustrated History of Hymns," by Rev. Edwin M. Long, author of several hymns, contains much that teaches what some Protestants deny. One story, which I found on opening the book, is on page 449 and is in brief this: In 1826 five missionaries, the wives of three and several children were in a wreck off the coast of Antigua. When the storm arose the little son of one of the missionaries gave out a verse of a hymn commencing:

"Though waves and storms go o'er my head."
and when it had been sung the child delivered an address on the shipwreck of Jonah and the author says a holy inspiration come over the child and affected all who heard him.

The wife of one of the missionaries was the only one who was calm enough to pray and when she had done so she sang:

When passing through the watery deep
I asked in faith his promised aid,
The waves an awful distance keep
And shrink from my devoted head.
Fearless their violence I dare
They cannot harm for God is there.

Sad to say, she was the only one saved out of that party. On pages 303, 304 and 305 is the story of George Neumark, who was reduced to such dire straits in Hamburg in 1651 that he had to pawn his violincello, which had been his chief means of supporting life. Before parting with it he improvised a hymn and accompanied his voice on the instrument, in the pawnbroker's house. A passer-by was charmed with the sen-timent and music and sought a copy. When Neumark had accommodated him the stranger took him to his master, the Swedish embassador, who made him his secretary. His grat-

HYMNS THAT BETRAY.

itude to God for this interposition he put in the form of a hymn, one verse of which is:

> Leave God to order all thy ways
> And hope in Him whate'er betide,
> Thou'lt find him in the evil days,
> Thine all sufficient strength and guide.
> Who trusts in God's unchanging love,
> Builds on the rock that ne'er can move.

When asked if this was his own composition, Neumark answered· "Well, yes. I am the instrument, but God swept the strings."

This book contains over 600 pages and is replete with anecdotes and extracts from hymns in which the miraculous abounds. If these hymns and these anecdotes do not teach that the age of miracles has been extended to the gloaming of the nineteenth century and the dawn of the twentieth, what do they mean? If those who wrote the hymns and related the anecdotes do not mean that they believe God sets aside known laws or grants prayer by the operation of laws unknown to man they mean worse than nothing. If they do not believe in what is called the miraculous they are confessedly false teachers who are taking the name of God in vain—uttering blasphemy by praying God for favors they do not believe He will grant. I prefer to believe the best of the authors of both hymns and anecdotes and to also believe that those who attack Christian Science, on the assumed ground that the age of miracles is past, are endeavoring to obtain religious advantages on false pretenses. This is a serious charge, as I make it, because in the school of ethics in which I was trained it is blasphemous in employing sin to further the cause of religion. I acquit these zealous brethren of willful hypocrisy, remembering that there are, according to Robert Colyer, the great Unitarian, I think, two classes of hypocrites, the conscious and the unconscious. It will remain for any of the attacking party to adjust to himself the accusation of willful hypocrisy by persisting in attacks after his attention has been directed to his own error.

MISCELLANEOUS MYSTERIES.

A COLLECTION OF MARVELS THAT RANGE FROM THE SUBLIME TO THE ABSURD.

Some of the marvels grouped under this head may not be properly classed as Protestant, but all or nearly all indicate some degree of Protestant belief in present supernatural aid to man.

Dr. Edward Berdoe has an article in the Nineteenth Century of October, 1895, descriptive of a visit to the grotto of Lourdes. He says:

> This earnestness on the part of the worshipers, if it do not take heaven by storm, exalts the whole organism and serves, of itself, to explain much of the thaumaturgy.

He also says:

> As Christianity has no monopoly of faith healing, we may imagine what it is which underlies all these phenomena. To set them aside as silly talk and priestly frauds is to betray the non-scientific mind. So universal a thaumaturgy implies a basis of fact which we must not despise. Professor Charcot has lent the great weight of his authority to the statement that faith-cure is an ideal method, since it oftens attains its end after all other means have failed.

Dr. Berdoe then cites M. Littre in "Fragment de Medicine

Retrospective," where he describes seven miracles wrought at the tomb of St. Louis and atempts to give a pathological interpretation of them, which Dr. Berdoe does not expressly endorse. He closes his article by saying that the scientific view of miracles of healing is no detraction from the power of prayer: "God ever works by natural laws; we use the word 'miracles' for the effect of natural laws which we do not understand." His closing lines are these:

> If the cure be wrought, what matters it to the happy invalid who, like Marie in M. Zola's novel, jumps from her wheel chair and, trailing it behind her, joins the procession of thanksgivers—whether the cure is wrought by the touch of a divine hand or the overpowering influence of a great idea on the nervous system.

BOEHME'S MYSTICISM.

Though mysticism and miracle-ism are not identical, they are nearly so in some cases. Jacob Boehme, the German mystic writer of the seventeenth century, did not pretend to perform miracles but to have witnessed many, and the fact that he had a large following among even well educated non-Catholics, shows that Protestants in Germany were not unanimous in the opinion that miracles were things of a past age. Even in England he had followers and his writings were translated by William Law, an eminent English clergyman. Law was an author of the so-called mystic school of his day but, though discountenanced by the established church, the Wesley brothers acknowledge that they derived great benefit from his "Serious Call to a Devout and Holy Life."

MISCELLANEOUS MYSTERIES.

A biography of Boehme, translated by Franz Hartmann, M. D., and published in 1891 in London, shows that Boehme, while a herder of cattle in his boyhood, had been guided by a vision to a cave where he found a pot of gold. Deeming the gold and the vision the result of a satanic plot, he fled without the treasure. A few years later, while an apprentice to a shoemaker, a mysterious stranger appeared to him, paid an extraordinary price for a pair of shoes, called him by name and revealed to him his future greatness, and admonished him to read the Bible, in which he would find comfort. He continued to have visions and, between 1612 and 1624, he wrote many books describing what he saw in those visions.

EVIDENCE OF MIRACLES.

Bishop Douglas of the Church of England is quoted by a writer in Blackwood's Magazine for November, 1823, as to the rules respecting the evidence of miracles. They are only two in number, but the explanation is somewhat lengthy and the rules, etc., are here presented:

1. That whenever a fact can be ascribed, however remotely, to natural causes, any reference to Divine interposition is absolutely excluded.

2. Whenever the testimony affords ground even for a suspicion of fraud, it must be rejected entirely and at once.

A suspicion of fraud is entertained:

1. If the accounts of the alleged miracles were not published to the world till long after the time when they are said to have been performed.

2. If the accounts were published at a distance

from the place where the miraculous agency was supposed to be manifested.

3. If at the time when and the place where they are said to have happened, they have been suffered to pass without due examination.

AS TO INSPIRATION.

Inspiration is a word over whose meaning a vast amount has been written. It is employed here in the sense of an extraordinary or divine agency by which God operates on the minds of teachers, speakers and writers, who are thus taught or guided how to teach, speak and write. This I find to be the sense in which the term is employed by people who attribute to certain preachers or religious teachers more than human power or wisdom.

Inspiration is a difficult term to define. The definition of the dictionaries will hardly do, because nearly every religious body gives to it a little different meaning. Some regard a preacher as inspired when he becomes excited and gives expression to unusual ideas; some regard the authors of new doctrine and dogma as inspired; some so regard a person who feels impelled to undertake any religious or philanthropic work and brings to his aid such zeal and enthusiasm as awakens like zeal and enthusiasm as well as liberality in others. While these variations of definitions do not vary so widely as to be inconsistent, they serve to illustrate the latitude taken by those who use the word in application to the talents or deeds of those whom they admire or whose cause they espouse. It seems not to make much difference whether the person thus regarded as inspired be poet, patriot, preacher, soldier, explorer or mere

MISCELLANEOUS MYSTERIES.

politician. If he acts or speaks with fervor on "my" side he is inspired; if on the other, "he hath a devil." In either case the mere notion of inspiration is the same. The only difference of opinion is as to the source.

Thousands regarded Wesley as inspired and the thousands have grown into millions in the present century. Within the memory of living men, women and children, Moody, Hammond, Fay Mills and others have been or are regarded as inspired, yet followers of each think Mrs. Mary B. Eddy impious because they say she believes her discovery of Christian Science a revelation or the result of inspiration. Mrs. Eddy makes no claim to any inspiration that might not come to any person who would undertake and pursue a course of study such as she underwent in her search for light on the power that healed her.

SPECIOUS ORTHODOX REASONING.

A fair example of the reasoning on which is based the assumption that the age of miracles ceased with the lives of the apostles, is found in Rev. Richard Watson's Biblical and Theological Dictionary, London, 1861. In that work the age of miracles is regarded as having closed with the second century. The argument is substantially this: Peter and Paul died between the years 66 and 67 of our era and John about the close of the first century. They may have imparted the gift of working miracles to others who may have survived to the end of the century and that the gift was not renewed by its "blessed author."

The defect of this reasoning is plain. It is reasoning only so far as the transmission by the three apostles named are concerned. From that point it is pure assumption that the successors did not and could not convey to others what had been conveyed to them.

THE PRAYER GAUGE.

Some twenty-five years ago Prof. Tyndall proposed a prayer test which was at the time made the subject of much newspaper joking as the "prayer gauge." Tyndall proposed that a certain number of sick persons be selected as subjects of prayer for recovery of health and that the number who recovered, under certain conditions, should be regarded as showing the efficacy or idleness of prayer.

Among those who took serious notice of this challenge was Rev. R. L. Dabney, Professor of Divinity in the Union Theological Seminary of the Presbyterian Church of the South and subsequently of the University of Texas. Prof. Dabney devotes a somewhat lengthy chapter to Tyndall's taunt, in which he shows that his church believes that prayers are answered and the blessings prayed for are granted if the petitioner does not "ask amiss."

SHAKER MARVELS.

F. W. Evans is the author of a history of the Shakers in which several miraculous occurrences are recorded. As Shakers are not regarded as Evangelical Christians, to quote their miracles would not be fair in this work if they had not the endorsement of orthodox Protestants. This endorsement was strikingly given in the case of "Mother" Ann Lee, when arraigned for blasphemy in England. She was brought before four ministers of the established church on this charge and at their request spoke for four hours in foreign tongues. The

MISCELLANEOUS MYSTERIES.

clergymen were learned linguists and declared that she employed during those four hours seventy-two different tongues or dialects. The little volume from which this is taken is full of stories of miraculous happenings but, as they all rest on Shaker evidence, they are not cited.

One is so remarkable, however, that it is given for quantity. Evans says after the ministers had released Mother Ann and those who were arraigned with her the mob of ostensible Christians took them to a convenient spot and, having provided themselves with stones, they began pelting the Shakers. Though within easy range and the mob large, the stones fell harmlessly around the prisoners, not one of whom was hit. Some of the mob were terror stricken and fled at beholding the miracle and the rest slunk away.

CREDULITY OF SKEPTICS.

It may seem foreign to this work to mention the story of Heinrich Hensoldt, Ph. D., of his visit to the Grand Lama of Thibet. He tells it in the October Arena for 1894. It is only apropos of the credulity of the incredulous; of those who are skeptical on all subjects except their peculiar fads. Hensoldt's story is, in brief, that he found the "incarnate Buddha" to be a boy apparently about eight years old, "certainly not over nine," and he describes him as of wonderful beauty and intelligence. He continues:

The Dalai Lama's gaze was that of an adept of the highest order, and as I encountered those wonderful eyes I knew and felt that I was in the presence of one who could read my innermost thoughts. He addressed me in my native German and moreover in a dialect which I had not heard for many years and which he could not have acquired by any process known to ordinary mortals. This is all the more remarkable when it is considered that I had taken special precautions to conceal my nationality.

This is enough of Dr. Hensoldt's wonderful tale, which occupies not only several pages in the number here given, but extends into other numbers of the magazine. It is somewhat remarkable that nobody has to this day questioned Hensoldt's veracity in any publication that I have been able to see.

THE LORD PROVIDED.

Members of the Christian Church, commonly called 'Campbellite," will recall the case of John Smith, one of their early missionary preachers in what is now the Central West. He told of his reaching Campbell's Ferry, in Kentucky, I think, without money with which to pay for carrying himself and his horse across the river. While he was meditating what kind of appeal he could make to the ferryman, a woman came down a by-path, approached him, handed him a silver quarter dollar without a word of explanation and retired as silently as she came.

I have been unable to find this anecdote in print, but I have heard it so often that I assume it to be familiar to all the disciples of Alexander Campbell and that some of them have the verified form of the story. Smith always said that the Lord provided that quarter because he was informed that the ferryman hated preachers in general and Campbellites in particular and wouldn't have ferried him without the cash.

MISCELLANEOUS MYSTERIES.

DICTATION TO OMNIPOTENCE.

J. Boyd Kinnear, who is a sufficiently respectable writer to have his matter printed in the Contemporary Review of December, 1879, Vol. XXXVI, page 625, said regarding miraculous healing:

It cannot be a breach of natural laws if God should effect it (cure) by any laws as yet unknown to man, provided they are brought into play with no other agency than the motion of matter.

This is not quoted here for its logic, but to show that believers in orthodoxy, in which class Mr. Kinnear appears to be, did not all discredit miraculous healing. Mr. Kinnear's logic is principally remarkable for its absence in his attempt to dictate to omnipotence that He must work according to his (Kinnear's) specifications and confine himself to the "agency of the motion of matter." After thus attempting to limit the infinite, Mr. Kinnear enters upon an extensive argument to show that the physical miracles of the Bible were all performed in harmony with laws not yet discovered by man.

DISBELIEF AS ATHEISM.

James Gairdner, who is presumably an orthodox minister, says in the Contemporary Review for June, 1876:

They who do not believe in a direct personal agency in the ordinary uniformity can hardly be said to have any genuine belief in God, at all.

This is said in reply to a Dr. Carpenter, who, in the January number of the same periodical, attempted to explain away all supernatural agency in what are considered miracles. Mr. Gairdner asks:

Is it more superstitious to speak of certain phenomena, which none of us can understand, as cases of "demoniacal possession" than to call them lunacy?

WOULD PILLORY HUME.

David Hume, in giving reasons to a friend why he wrote his essay on miracles, says the idea occurred to him while conversing with a Jesuit at the college of La Fleche, in France. The Jesuit having told of a recent miracle, Hume disputed him. To his argument the Jesuit replied that it could have no solidity because it operated as much against the Gospels as the miracle. This conversation led to a train of thought, of which the essay was the result.

That the essay was regarded as of peculiar force is evident from an extract from Bishop Warburton's "railings," as an eminent prelate of the Church of England characterized them. Warburton said he was minded to "do justice to his arguments against miracles." What his idea of justice was may be judged from this, which follows closely on the words above quoted:

> But does he deserve this notice? Is he known amongst you? If his own weight keeps him down I should be sorry to contribute to his advancement except to the pillory.

What the essay was may be further inferred from the fact that it is difficult, according to apparently good authority, to find an edition of Hume's essays in England, from which that essay has not been omitted, though all good libraries in the United States contain unexpurgated editions. This opposition from people who scouted the idea that miracles were possible in their own day serves to show that their absurdity was as great as their intolerance.

A MORAVIAN EXAMPLE.

"Tales and Sketches of Christian Life in Different Lands and Ages" is the lengthy title to a small volume by Mrs. E. Charles, author of "The Schonberg-Cotta Family" and other semi-religious works. It depicts the rise of the sect known as United Brethren or Moravians. That part of the book opens with a conversation between Brother Gregory, the head of the sect in Bohemia, nearly forty years after the martyrdom of John Huss and his uncle, John Rockyzan, a secret leader of the same, though he was, by the choice of the people, archbishop of Prague, Bohemia, but unconfirmed by the Pope. Rockyzan desires to remain in the church the better to help the Brethren, but Gregory argues:

> We have no resource but to recognize those amongst us whom God has endowed with gifts of governing and teaching and to trust Him for the result. Our high-priest, our master, our bishop, our chief, is none else than the living Son of God; our canons His Word; our guide and counselor the Eternal Spirit.

Mrs. Charles' works were all apparently written for the entertainment and instruction of youth. Though they do not contain much in the way of stories of the miraculous, they contain much that tends to teach Divine interposition in favor of man for what appear to be rewards of righteousness or the promotion of pious purposes.

Mrs. Charles' works are by no means singular in this regard. Juvenile literature intended for propagation of faith generally contains so much that is miraculous in its nature that it became a by-word among scoffers in the form of jests about the wicked boy contradicting the books by escaping all manner of perils while violating the Sabbath, while the virtuous boy of the Sunday school books always died young.

VARIED MARVELS.

UNCLASSED WONDERS TAKEN FROM THE WRITINGS OF PIOUS PROTESTANTS AND OTHER AUTHORITIES.

In "Modern Doubt and Christian Belief" Dr. Christlieb, who is described elsewhere, relates an account of miracles that may almost be called modern. Dr. Christlieb tells of Hans Egede, the first evangelical missionary to Greenland, healing several natives, of grievous ailments, by miraculous means. He also cites, on a page close to that containing the Greenland story, instances of the miraculous provision for two missionaries in North America, Spangenberg and Zeisgeber. They were nearly famished while traveling through a wilderness, when they came to a clear stream.

Spangenberg bade his companion get out the fishing tackle and cast a line into the stream. Zeisgeber reminded him that it was the season when the fish had gone seaward and pointed to the water, in which not a fish was visible. Spangenberg told him to proceed, nevertheless, and he obeyed. The result was so successful that it is compared to the miraculous draft of fish in the gospel.

Christlieb also quotes from a memoir of Kleinschmidt, published in 1866, an incident of a Christian convert in South Africa, who, in 1858, instantly healed a comrade who was so wounded in both legs that he could not walk. The convert bade him, in the name of Jesus, to arise and walk, which the cripple instantly did.

Orthodox writers, as a rule, seem to have ignored all modern miracles. Ecclesiastical authority having once taken the ground that the age of miracles had passed, the majority of writers and lecturers seem to have bowed to the dogma and closed their eyes to what seem to be well authenticated facts. When one contemplates the studious efforts of even eminent theological teachers and historians to suppress facts which, to say the least in their support, are as well authenticated as the Gospels, it is no wonder that there is so little in collateral history to corroborate the evangelists.

Some of the most remarkable cases of miracles or wonders are related by infidel writers, apparently for the purpose of showing that while they were wonders they were not miracles in the sense that they were the result of Divine suspension of natural laws or were produced by special interposition of Providence for the occasion. In a book entitled "Supernatural Religion," and published by Longmans & Green, London, the author, whose name is not disclosed in either of the two volumes, devotes twenty-five pages to a summary of miracles related of and by Christians of later days than the apostles. Those attributed to Gregory are the most marvelous and in some respects far surpass any attributed to Jesus. One is that two brothers, having quarreled over the proprietary right to a lake, Gregory caused it to dry up and become a fertile field. In another he planted his staff at a spot where a river annually overflowed its banks and caused great loss of life and property.

The stick took root and became a tree, after which the river never overflowed.

Much space is devoted to the miracles asserted to have been wrought by St. Augustine, but in both cases the author only quotes to discredit these accounts, while such Christian writers as Bruce of Glasgow and Fisher of Yale University refer to "Catholic" miracles as unworthy of credit.

Hume in his essay on "Human Understanding of Miracles" relates several of the Jansenist, Abbe Paris. These he says were proved to the satisfaction of a large number of French cures (pastors) before a bishops' court in Paris under the eye of Cardinal Noailles, but Hume calls them impostures. Hume was an infidel, but in this was in harmony with many, in fact most of Christian authors and preachers.

The man known as the Abbe Paris was born in 1727 and was not a priest. He had received deacon's orders but was not satisfied with the papal bull "Unigenitus" and deemed it wrong to receive full ordination. He had resigned his patrimony to his brother in anticipation of taking orders and hence was very poor. He retired to a part of the city inhabited by other very poor people and supported himself by making stockings. His scanty earnings he shared with the poor, to whom he ministered in every way in his power. It was generally believed that his voluntary privations greatly shortened his life.

Though history shows that Protestant writers have, ever since the Reformation, made great efforts to destroy the belief in miracles, that belief has risen among them with great force and at comparatively brief intervals. The healings attributed to the Abbe Paris may be properly classed as Protestant, as may also the visions and prophesies of Isabel Vincent in France in 1686. Of those visions and prophesies little need be said here beyond the fact that the pastors of the fugitive and persecuted French Protestants believed them to have been inspired, and when a century later the French revolution occurred it was hailed as the fulfillment of one of her prophesies.

A LUTHERAN WITNESS.

Heinrich Steffens was enough of a literary light to have several pages devoted to him in "Outlines of German Literature," a book which reviews the work of typical German writers. He was won away from Lutheranism by "that negative school of German philosophy whose tendency is to destroy the foundations of religion," as the compilers of the work say. Steffens was reconverted, however, and in his work, "How I Became a Lutheran Once More," he says:

> Despite all the progress of science, an obscure belief in the supernatural underlies all our clearer notions, induced from observations respecting only the ordinary course of events.
>
> * * *
>
> This experience, founded on acquaintance with the ordinary course of events, and most valuable in its way, does not warrant us in affirming that such laws of nature as we know are absolute and supreme. Where our own reasonings are confronted with an event, for which our limited experience can assign no adequate cause, it is fair to conclude that, as the cause of the event itself is for us mys-

terious, so the circumstances attending that event may be mysterious also.

* * *

We cannot destroy faith in the supernatural. Driven from one place it will reappear in another. It might be better to find for it a safe home, a proper sphere, and this home, I would suggest, is found in Christianity.

MAN ABOVE NATURE.

Rev. Lucius Curtis had an article in the Andover Review for August, 1892, on "Man Above Nature," in which he combats the positions of Spencer, Huxley et id and, after reviewing the power manifested by man, says:

We have now seen that the economy of Nature which gives to the highest order of force on a given plane the prerogative to rule all the forces of that plane by its own law, assigns to man, as having rational energy, the prerogative to rule all the forces of his organism by the law of rational life. We have seen also that this is not the law of any natural force, but a spiritual law for the direction of natural forces, and that this has sway only as it is freely accepted and administered by a personal power through functions that transcend those of nature and are spiritual in their character.

INFIDEL TESTIMONY.

HUXLEY AND LECKY ON THE REALITY OF WONDERFUL CURES.

Prof. T. H. Huxley, in the Popular Science Monthly of September, 1889, in an article on the same subject, speaks of the wonderful work of George Fox, the founder of the Quakers, whom he compares to the Apostle Paul for what he did and endured and whose veracity and honesty he fully endorses. The most wonderful of his works is quoted from his autobiography. It is of the healing of an insane woman for whom the medical men could do nothing. She was so violent that it required many persons to hold her and a doctor was about to "let her blood" when Fox interfered, bade people release her and restored her to sanity—instantly, it is implied. The woman thus healed is said to have "lived long in the truth."

The same magazine in April, 1878, quotes Lecky, the historian, thus:

There is no contradiction involved in the belief that spiritual beings of power and wisdom immeasurably transcending our own exist, or that, existing, they might, by the normal exercise of their powers, perform feats as far surpassing the understanding of the most gifted of mankind, as the electric telegraph and the prediction of an eclipse surpass the faculties of a savage.

This remark of Lecky is applied to a debate in the Prussian parliament over the Marpingen miracles, but those miracles, being of the discredited Catholic class, only serve here

INFIDEL TESTIMONY. 153

to show that Lecky was more liberal than his countrymen in general toward those whose belief differed from their own.

The London Saturday Review, from which Lecky's words were copied, remarked of miracle-cures that, whatever may be thought of them, the records of cures of supposed hydrophobia by appeal to the imagination by religious relics, were well attested. It quotes Sir James Stephens in attestation of such healings, Lecky on other miracles and even Voltaire to the same effect.

SKEPTICS TAXING CREDULITY.

It will not escape the critical reader that these and nearly all other hypotheses advanced by men who wrote several centuries after the events, draw as heavily upon human credulity as do the Gospel accounts of miracles.

Then these critics, who disbelieve the Gospel as to miracles, discredit each other by each offering a different hypothesis. Some seem willing to believe in some of the miracles or in the miraculous to a degree. This naturally causes the question: "If a miracle of lesser degree can be wrought, why not of any degree? If one can believe in the supernatural in any degree, why not believe in it to any extent?" It would seem reasonable that if what is viewed as natural law could be suspended to permit the immaculate conception and birth of Jesus, it could also be suspended to raise the dead. If the maxim of common law is as good in physics or metaphysics as in jurisprudence, then either all the Gospel accounts of miracles are true or none of them are. This maxim, which is the crystallization of the wisdom of lawyers, and is founded on the observations during centuries, says: "False in one thing, false in all."

TRACTARIAN MIRACLES.

THE AMERICAN TRACT SOCIETY'S "SKETCHES FROM LIFE" CONTAIN THEM.

A volume of 515 pages, published by the American Tract Society in 1871, and entitled "Sketches From Life," contains a large number of stories illustrative of the efficacy of prayer. In at least two places of the volume the authors of certain articles say the age of miracles is past, even though the incidents related are in the nature, at least, of miracles. One story, entitled "The Cut Finger," is either that of a miracle or else it is a falsehood.

The story is that a boy four years old had the ill luck to have one of his fingers cut off in a hay cutter. The mother clapped it on and kept it there until a surgeon arrived. The doctor bound up the wound in the hope of saving the finger and directed that the dressing be not disturbed for six days. During that time the child suffered greatly and when the doctor removed the bandages the finger dropped off. The mother replaced it and the doctor told her he would call with another surgeon soon to see what could be done. They did not arrive until twenty-four hours later, when, directed by his senior and superior in skill, the doctor again dressed the wound, and more skillfully, it is inferred rather than asserted.

All the while the mother was praying fervently and incessantly for the restoration of the child whom she had des-

TACTARIAN MIRACLES.

tined for the pulpit. When again the bandages were removed the severed finger was found to have reunited itself to the hand, but had not healed straight and the surgeon advised that it be amputated. The mother resisted, and when the story was written the boy had become a man and approved his mother's action. The author of the story intimates the opinion a miracle was not wrought, but says none could convince the pious mother that her prayers had not done more than the skill of the surgeons.

The volume contains in all nearly 200 stories of answers to prayers by which those who prayed were relieved of sickness, debt and other distress; of marvelous conversions of criminals and drunkards and even of a pirate who became so penitent that he surrendered when, but for hearing a woman at prayer on a vessel he had captured, he would have slain the whole crew and passengers.

A sketch of the life of Francis Marion, the rough rider of South Carolina, says God saved him from death by shipwreck for his greater work, that of aiding in winning independence for America.

Another miracle story is that of Jacob Manfred, whose residence and the age in which he lived are unmentioned. While wealthy he adopted a friendless boy, who, when he grew up, disappeared. Manfred lost his wealth when old age made him and his wife decrepit. Just as a rude, unfeeling officer was about to take the poor old couple to the workhouse, a stranger appeared, announced himself to be the adopted boy who had won wealth abroad and returned to provide for his benefactor and benefactress in their declining years.

PROTESTANT MIRACLES.

Like the majority of the stories related in Mr. Schuh's volume, which is mentioned elsewhere in this work, those in this sketch book are not so authenticated as to command much attention. Were it published by a less responsible or less well known concern than the American Tract Society, little heed would be paid to them. They are all written in a style that shows them to have been intended for juvenile reading, and as they all inculcate a belief that prayers are answered by the granting of the petitions of suppliants, it seems conclusive evidence that the Protestant sects that maintain the American Tract Society are teaching that the age of miracles is not past.

A LAYMAN'S MIRACLES.

VALENTINE GREATRAKES' FEATS AS RECORDED IN THE ROYAL SOCIETY MEMOIRS.

Valentine Greatrakes, who was born in Ireland in 1628, is accredited with the miraculous gift of curing the King's evil (scrofula) by the combined means of laying on of hands and prayer. In the "Imperial Dictionary of Universal Biography," edited by a number of men whose learning is attested by the addenda of M. A., LL.D., etc., to their names, Greatrakes is said to have performed many marvelous cures. The article in the dictionary which is credited to Birch's Memoirs of the Royal Society, says Greatrakes was a man of unimpeachable integrity, incapable of perpetrating an imposture. Though he cured vast numbers of poor people he failed to heal Lady Conway, though he made a journey to England for the purpose. He did not exercise his power for gain, as he had an ample estate, which was generally crowded with people seeking his aid after he made it generally known that he possessed such wonderful powers. His practice fell into disrepute in England in 1666, after his examination before the Royal Society, and though he survived until about 1690, the chronicler of the society says no more was heard of him after 1666. The account does not say at what time Greatrakes began to exercise his powers, but leaves it to be inferred, from the fact that he first communicated his belief in himself to his wife. Let it be assumed that this was when he was thirty years old, or in 1658, and it would appear that he must have practiced in the neighborhood of eight years.

LIMITING GOD'S POWER.

PECULIAR THEORY OF FRANCES POWER COBBE ON ANSWER TO PRAYER.

Frances Power Cobbe, who has published several volumes on moral and religious subjects within a few years, issued in 1883 a volume entitled "Religious Duty." In this is a chapter devoted to prayer, in the opening of which she repeats what she said in her "Theory of Morals," viz: "That the law of spirit is that light and strength are bestowed on man by God according as the latter places himself further from or nearer to their source." She then proceeds:

The plant which is sickly, weak and white, growing in the darkness, acquires health and verdure when we bring it into the sunshine. The magnetic bar which has lost its power regains it when we hang it in the plane of the meridian. Thus (whatever other prayer may be), the prayer for spiritual good is the direct mode of obtaining assistance to our virtue, in accordance with the fixed laws of Providence.

* * *

It will be seen here that I assume it to be proved that there is an actual answer given by God to our requests for His assistance. I assume that the strength which comes to us in prayer is not merely a subjective phenomenon, the strength acquired by the will by its own act of excercise. * * * * * * * *

LIMITING GOD'S POWER.

There is a natural supply for spiritual as for corporeal wants, so we have spiritual facilities to lay hold on God and supply spiritual wants.

This last sentence the lady attributes to Theodore Parker, in a footnote. After arguing the correctness of these views she says:

All this is natural, normal. It is not a miracle that the Omnipresent is close to us, that the Omniactive moves our hearts. It is not strange that the Infinite Father, who bears us in his everlasting arms, should supply the cravings of our immortal souls while He feeds the ravens and gives the young lions their prey. It would be a miracle if it were otherwise.

The argument, then, stands thus: He who doubts that God hears prayer, denies that we have proof of the fact. But what proof would satisfy him? If he say "None," this would imply that there is an essential absurdity in the case, but we must call on him to point out the absurdity since we cannot see it. But if he admit that the thing is not, in itself, absurd and self-contradictory, then it seems to me he cannot ask any other proof than exactly that which abounds,—namely, the unanimous testimony of spiritual persons to the efficacy of prayer.

The gifted authoress carries out this idea, but confines it strictly to prayer for spiritual gifts—the prayer for light and grace and says:

To the soul which has reached that stage of spiritual life wherein such culmination of worship takes

PROTESTANT MIRACLES.

place, it is revealed that God does actually hear, accept and bless, ay, in a certain sense (if we may dare symbolize His awful nature) desire the prayer of His child.

After this and much more of evidence that she has a very full appreciation of the majesty, sublimity and omniscience of God, Miss Cobbe on the next page proceeds to put a limit on the power of Omnipotence thus:

Does philosophy warrant us to expect that God will grant any prayer for physical good,—for abundant harvests, favorable weather, recovery from sickness or so on?

This question she answers in the negative in several pages in which she employs arguments that, were one to take the trouble to remodel them, would be equally forcible against her position that God hears and answers prayer for spiritual good. She argues that to answer such prayers would be to make His laws operate unequally and hence unjustly; which is not to be considered. In fortification of this position she says "prayer begins where science stops and as science advances prayer retreats."

Miss Cobbe's orthodoxy, in this respect, is very evident and she admits that God made everything and governs everything, but still denies that He has any other power over the physical world than that indicated in those laws of nature of which man is informed. That is not her way of expressing the opinion. She employs some very subtle reasoning, based upon what she knows, in an effort to prove that God has no powers of which human philosophers are unaware. Miss Cobbe was not orthodox in the usually accepted sense. She underwent

LIMITING GOD'S POWER.

great tribulation in consequence of her meditations on religious subjects and, after reading and studying widely on the subject and many phases of it, she became an ardent admirer of the late Theodore Parker and published an edition of his writings. Miss Cobbe is an Irish woman of high education and seems to have inherited ample means to enable her to pursue her studies all her life. Though she is not an orthodox Protestant, these extracts from her writings are quoted for what they are worth.

PHILOSOPHERS' OPINIONS.

SOME EMINENT SCIENTISTS WHO HAVE REBUKED SCIENTIFIC SKEPTICISM.

In the course of my researches I have consulted few works that treated of spiritualism, but have avoided them as foreign to my purpose. By a singular error in the transposition of figures in a memorandum of library numbers I got a little work by Alfred Russell Wallace, an English author of some note, "On Miracles and Modern Spiritualism." The first thing that struck me in this book was a page of quotations, which I copy, viz:

A presumptuous skepticism that rejects facts without examination of their truth is, in some respects, more injurious than unquestioning credulity.—Humboldt.

One good experiment is of more value than the ingenuity of a brain like Newton's. Facts are more useful when they contradict, than when they support, received theories.—Sir Humphrey Davy.

The perfect observer in any department of science will have his eyes, as it were, opened, that they may be struck at once by any occurrence which, according to received theories, ought not to happen, for these are the facts which serve as clues to new discoveries.—Sir John Herschell.

PHILOSOPHERS' OPINIONS.

Before experience itself can be used with advantage, there is one preliminary step to make which depends entirely upon ourselves: It is the absolute dismissal and clearing of the mind of all prejudice, and the determination to stand or fall by the result of a direct appeal to facts in the first instance, and of strict logical deduction from them afterwards.—Sir John Herschell.

With regard to the miracle question, I can only say that the word "impossible" is not, to my mind, applicable to matters of philosophy. That the possibilities of nature are infinite is an aphorism with which I am wont to worry my friends.—Prof. Huxley.

I cannot resist the impulse to here remark that those clergymen and other writers who have employed the methods that skeptical philosophers have used against all miracles, in their battling against the belief in modern thaumaturgy, that it would be better for their reputations as logicians were they to also adopt the liberality of the "infidel philosophers."

Mr. Wallace devotes much attention to Hume's account of the Jansenist miracles and exposes some glaring contradictions in his work. Placing the contradictory passages sufficiently near to make their incongruity striking, he shows the "infidel" historian and philosopher to have indulged in what is characterized in the American trick politician as "faking."

DIVINE WRATH.

WHAT ORTHODOX PEOPLE BELIEVE OF GOD'S VENGEANCE ON INFIDELS.

Take up a volume of sermons by T. DeWitt Talmage and see if you do not find evidences that he believed in modern miracles. In a volume published in 1886 is one on the topic: "Why are Satan and Sin Permitted?" In this he expresses the opinion that God's interposition brought about the downfall of "Boss" Tweed of New York City and the death by accident of William the Conqueror. In the same sermon he speaks of the establishment of an infidel college in that indefinite region, "the far West. It languished a short time and then the Presbyterians gained possession of it, and Talmage attributes the failure and change of ownership to God's influence if not direct interposition.

This recalls what was uttered from many pulpits after the massacre at New Ulm, Minnesota, during the Indian war in the fifth decade of this century. New Ulm was settled by German infidels, who made a law that no minister of the Gospel should be suffered to remain in that place. When the Indians destroyed the town Christian ministers in large numbers, and in many states, said God used the Indians as instruments of his wrath to rebuke or revenge the infidelity of the people who wouldn't suffer a church to be built or a minister to reside in the town. This sentiment was expressed at the meeting of the Dakota Mission conference of the M. E. Church in 1884, and was not disputed by any of the assembled ministers.

MARK OF ARETHUSA.

A PROTESTANT HISTORIAN ACCEPTS ONE ACCOUNT OF POST-APOSTOLIC MIRACLES.

Millman's History of Christianity, pp. 25 to 35, contains an account of Mark of Arethusa being accused of having destroyed a Jewish temple and being ordered to rebuild it. As Mark was as poor as other early Christian apostles, the order could not be carried out, but the Jews undertook the work themselves. While they were engaged in clearing the ruins a series of explosions occurred which drove the workers out repeatedly and defeated them in their efforts to rebuild.

On page 27 the learned historian indulges in reflections on the relative credibility of accounts of miracles addressed to terror and those that appeal to calmer emotions. It is evident that his conclusion is in favor of the latter class, while he does not discredit the other. Further along in his work, page 165 and beyond, he quotes Augustine and Ambrose to the effect that miracles had ceased during their early days, but he also shows that both of these fathers professed to have wrought miracles.

In doing this Millman, like White and some others, seems to forget that they have proved both sides of the question, as he expresses no doubt of the genuineness of the history he quotes. Those who argue after that fashion may never have

PROTESTANT MIRACLES.

read the rule that what proves equally well for both sides proves nothing.

In this case Millman's position is only valuable as the testimony of an adverse witness giving unwilling evidence that he and his confreres make an exception to what they would have people believe is the invariable rule, whenever they find miracles that strike their fancy.

A MORMON MIRACLE.

A DAY OF FASTING RESTORES HEALTH WHERE THE DOCTORS ADMIT THAT THEY ARE POWERLESS.

As I have included in this collection of wonders a few miracles that I have classed as non-religious and some from the Shakers, who, being Unitarians, are not considered Evangelical, I may also be indulged in making a Mormon miracle a feature of the work The story reached me after my first "copy" was in the hands of the printer and I have not had time to get the particulars or have the main story verified by the authorities. My informant is the person who taught the public school in Annabella, Sevier county, Utah; a non-Mormon and not a member of any other church. The story in brief is this:

Mrs. Hattie Stewart had given birth to a child in 1896 and all went apparently well. After she had been confined to her bed six weeks I first heard of the case on the death of the child. I visited Mrs. Stewart at the request of her friends and found her greatly wasted and almost in a state of exhaustion. She lingered under a doctor's care nearly three months and then the physicians gave up the case as one for whom their skill was of no avail.

At this point the bishop and elders of Annabella began visiting Mrs. Stewart and appointed a fast day for the purpose of benefiting her. I heard of the appointment and gladly joined in the effort, knowing it could do no harm to either patient or fasters and feeling that if prayer could be efficacious it would be as likely to be so in her case as any. I explained the fast day and its purpose to the children and they became enthusiastic in the cause.

When the day arrived, I think it was the day after I announced it to them, fully two-thirds of my thirty odd pupils came to school fasting. They didn't even drink water, and out of the 350 adult inhabitants or thereabouts, fully 300 fasted half the day and 250 until 4 p. m., the hour appointed.

Among the few non-Mormons in the village there were some who secretly scouted the idea that the fasting could have any effect and some declared that the fasters would harm themselves. Though I remained there several months after the event, I heard of no ill effects, while I know that Mrs. Stewart recovered her health and the people of Annabella know it and believe her recovery is due to their prayers.

Although the extraordinary events recorded in this chapter cannot be called Protestant, they are so interesting in themselves and are so nearly miraculous as to merit a place in this work as contradicting the assumption that the age of miracles is past.

WHAT ARE MIRACLES?

SOME DEFINITIONS AND EXPLANATIONS OF THE TERM BY DIFFERENT AUTHORITIES.

Lexicographers define miracles as events or effects contrary to the established course of things or the known laws of nature; supernatural events or events transcending the ordinary laws by which the universe is governed.

Among the ablest defenders of the miraculous origin of Christianity is Archbishop Trench of Dublin. On page 9 of his "Notes on the Miracles of Our Lord," a work republished in the United States by the Tibbals Book Company of New York, the Archbishop thus defines a miracle:

> An extraordinary Divine casualty, and not that ordinary which we acknowledge everywhere and in everything; belongs then to the essence of a miracle; powers of God other than those which have always been working; such indeed as most seldom or never have been working before. The unresting activity of God which at other times hides and conceals itself behind the veil of what we term natural laws, does in the miracle unveil itself; it steps out from its concealment and the hand which works is laid bare. Beside and beyond the ordinary operations of nature, higher powers (higher, not as coming from a higher source, but as bearing upon higher end) intrude and make themselves

felt even at the very springs and sources of her power. On page 11 he further speaks of miracles thus:

But while the miracle is not thus nature, so neither is it against nature. That language, however uncommon, is wholly unsatisfactory, which speaks of these wonderful works of God as violations of natural law. Beyond nature, beyond and above the nature which we know, they are, but not contrary to it.

What says Christian Science of miracles? On page 582 of Science and Health they are defined as "divinely natural." On page 28 miracles are treated of as in accordance with God's law, a demonstration of "the superiority of spiritual power over material resistance." On page 249 miracles are said to be impossible in science, which teaches that the highest manifestation of life or truth is not supernatural, but from the divine nature whose laws are superior to material laws, and miracles are but the natural demonstrations of this Divine power."

Christian Science holds that the miracles of Jesus did not especially belong to a dispensation that has ended, but that they illustrate a divine principle that is always operative, but which human theories cannot explain or interpret.

AFRAID OF A WORD.

In most of the works from which I have quoted or to which I have referred as of orthodox Protestant authority, there seems to be a studied avoidance of the word "miracle" as applied to modern events that come under the definitions quoted herein. It seems to have become a settled habit with those who defend

WHAT ARE MIRACLES?

the miraculous origin of Christianity, yet declare that the age of miracles is past. In the course of an argument in support of the miracles of the Gospel against those who assailed them, Archbishop Trench says on page 49 of his work on "The Miracles of Our Lord:"

The existence of false cycles of miracles should no more cast suspicion upon all or cause to doubt those which present themselves with marks of the time, than the appearance of a parhelion fore-running the sun should cause us to deny that he was traveling up from beneath the horizon, for which, rather, it is an evidence.

This argument the prelate seems to think powerful against the heathen philosophers and those modern infidels who employ the alleged miracles of Apollonius of Tyana to discredit the Gospel accounts of those performed by Jesus of Nazareth. The learned prelate does not seem to have foreseen that his argument would ever be employed by those whom the priests of his church now condemn as deluders or the deluded.

WHY THEY ARE INCENSED.

EVIDENCES THAT FEAR, NOT DISBELIEF, CAUSES ATTACKS ON CHRISTIAN SCIENCE.

The Church would never have attacked Christian Science if its author had confined her efforts to the healing of disease, and the doctors would not have assailed it had she simply labored to teach a new theory in religion or organize a new sect. Doctors and ministers do not agree well, as classes, but as Mrs. Eddy has invaded the fields of both they join forces to attack her. The ministers are rather less unmanly than the doctors in their attacks because they generally make open assaults, while the doctors act covertly, through legislatures, coroners' juries and through the bigotry of the ignorant.

In this the history of Christian Science resembles the early history of Christianity. If Jesus had not attempted to reform the religion of His day the priests would not have denounced Him. The priests and lawyers of that day possessed nearly all the learning and they seem to have been afflicted with fear like that which is taking possession of the priests and doctors of to-day. The physicians of apostolic days do not seem to have joined in the persecution of Christ and his followers. The doctors with whom Jesus disputed in the synagogue were not physicians, but teachers—doctors of the law—or lawyers like Saul of Tarsus. It is fair to assume that Jesus did not interfere with

WHY THEY ARE INCENSED.

their financial interests in healing the sick and raising the dead or they would have aided in raising the mob that insisted on Jesus being punished under the civil law for treason, when the real complaint against him was heresy, of which the Roman law took no jurisdiction. The heresy consisted of efforts to make the Jewish religion practical instead of theoretical; to make it a religion of deeds as well as of creed.

There is nothing your average priest, preacher or minister dreads and hates more than an attempt to reduce religion to practice, unless it is the person who makes the attempt and demands that the preachers exemplify their sincerity by their practices. This is about as true of the present as of the past. The reasons they do not instigate mobs to persecute Mrs. Eddy and her followers are that the people are not as easily led as they were in those old days; that the clergy are not united either as to what constitutes heresy or what constitutes true religion, and that the laws of the land forbid. The last reason is the result of the too free exercise of priestly influence in causing persecution for opinion's sake and is not attributable to the reduction to practice of that precept of Jesus that the greatest of virtues is charity.

SCOURGED TO THE PULPIT.

A NONOGENARIAN MINISTER WHOM GOD CONSTRAINED TO ENTER THE PULPIT.

Rev. J. C. Holbrook, D. D., LL.D., now over ninety years old, was for more than half a century a Congregational minister. He was the first editor of the Congregational Herald of Chicago, where he was also pastor of a church during two years or more. He issued in 1897 "Recollections of a Nonogenarian," in which is incorporated an autobiography. In this the venerable divine, who has for several years lived in retirement in Stockton, California, says his mother's prayers caused him to become a minister. He describes his career up to his entry of the ministry and says "though the answer (to her prayers) was delayed awhile, were at last answered and for that I shall be ever grateful to her and to Him who answers prayer."

Further along he tells of his success as a young man in politics and the probability of its continuance had he continued. "But God had other and better things in regard to me." And in returning to the subject he repeats: "As I have said, God had something better for me than a political career."

On page 42 he says of his membership in the church of Dr. Lyman Beecher of Boston: "It was part of God's appointed preparation of me for my subsequent professional career."

On page 53, in treating of the successful establishment of an insane asylum at Brattleboro, Vt., in which enterprise he was an active agent, he says:

But this is only one of a multitude of illustrations

SCOURGED TO THE PULPIT.

which history affords that, in the providence of God, vast and beneficial results have flowed from what seemed to human eyes very insignificant beginnings. Let us not "despise the day of small things." No benevolent act, however small, is performed in vain, and we may confidently expect the blessing of God on any enterprise undertaken for His glory and the good of mankind.

Dr. Holbrook has the deep satisfaction of having been the first person to introduce Henry Ward Beecher to the public. That was after his return to Vermont from Boston, when, after engaging O. S. Fowler to lecture on temperance, that gentleman, who had as yet no fame, recommended his college classmate, Beecher, to whom Mr. Holbrook paid $10, the first money young Beecher had ever earned as a lecturer.

Some passages in Dr. Holbrook's book are very affecting, especially those in which he tells of the death of his sons and his first wife; his suffering from nostalgia; his determination to return to the East from Davenport, Iowa, whither he had migrated with the intention of becoming a farmer. Regarding all this, after saying he decided to return to the East, he says:

But such was not the will of God. He had been preparing me for a life-work different from that I anticipated, and in part for this purpose broke up my family.

And now occurred, in accordance with His plans, one of the most important providential interpositions in my affairs, of which I have so many to record, and which changed my whole subsequent life.

PROTESTANT MIRACLES.

Dr. Holbrook then tells how he was led to Dubuque by a circuitous route and a rare combination of circumstances that culminated in a call to the pastorate of a Presbyterian church; its change to Congregational; his success there from 1842 until 1852; his marriage to his second wife, to whom he says he was "most providentially directed, as fifty-two years of experience in our after united life have abundantly proven."

The room to give all of the venerable doctor's views on special providences cannot be spared here. These extracts are sufficient to show that one eminently respectable Congregationalist, who has heard two generations of Beechers preach; whose devotion to his church has earned him his learned titles from two different colleges, believes in the miraculous and has left enduring evidence of that belief. As the book was published at the request of the Monday Club of San Francisco and vicinity, which club is composed of orthodox ministers; which request was supplemented by like requests from other ministers, it cannot but be regarded as sound orthodoxy. One reason why so much space is devoted to it here is that a minister of the denomination to which Dr. Holbrook belongs, and apparently an intimate friend of the venerable divine, recently indulged in a lengthy attack upon Christian Science and derided its author as "ill-brained and ill-trained" for expressing opinions that to an impartial reader would seem less inconsistent with reverence for the omniscience and loving kindness of God than Dr. Holbrook's idea that God deprived his first wife and second child of life in order to constrain him to devote himself to preaching the Gospel.

DEBT PAID MIRACULOUSLY.

It would appear from the character of some books that are published for the use of preachers that they are expected to believe stories of the miraculous even without the verification prescribed by good theological authorities who doubt. "Anecdotes Illustrative of New Testament Texts" is the title of one volume of the "Clerical Library," published by A. C. Armstrong & Son, New York, "for the clergy and students of all denominations." To judge from the appearance of the volume I found in a public library, it had been thoroughly used by one clergyman, who marked several passages. No name of author or compiler appears and few of the anecdotes have even the name of those to whom they are attributed as experiences.

In this volume are numerous stories of answer to prayer wherein the petitioners were delivered from evils of various kinds. One, attributed to Rev. Frederick Robinson, residence not given, tells how he escaped a flogging at school by the power of prayer, and this is attributed to Dr. Krummacher of Elberfeld, Prussia. who has written considerable theological matter:

A poor man in the neighborhood was sitting at his door early in the morning, weeping. His heart cried to heaven, for he was expecting an officer to distrain him for debt. While thus sitting a little bird fluttered into his cottage. The man closed the door and caught the bird, which at once began to sing what he imagined to be the melody of his favorite hymn, "Fear thou not when darkness reigns," and the thought comforted him.

Suddenly a knock came at the door and a servant of a lady came in to recover the escaped bird. In a few minutes after he surrendered the sweet singer, the servant returned with the thanks of his mistress and a sum of money. When the officer came the debtor handed him the money—the exact amount of the debt, saying: "Here is the amount. God has sent it to me. Leave me in peace."

BELIEF IN 1899.

MOODY AND CALIFORNIAN CLERGYMEN ON PRAYER FOR RAIN.

The great valleys of California suffered a severe drouth during the grain season of 1898 and farmers lost vast amounts. The winter of 1898-9 threatened another season of drouth. Only five inches of water had fallen for the season 1897-8 and up to the close of 1898 no more had fallen at the point of average precipitation.

Prayers went up in nearly all parts of the state for rain, but what fell previous to March 15, 1899, was only enough to aggravate the fears and anxieties of the farmers. On the 15th rain began falling and continued to fall in generous volume until the average was exceeded by about 10 per cent. By the close of March the despondency of the farmers and business men, who are dependent more upon agricultural success than on any other industry, was turned to hope and joy.

On the 25th of March the Sunday Bulletin of San Francisco published the views of a number of clergymen on the efficacy of prayer for rain. D. L. Moody, the world-renowned evangelist, was among those interviewed, he being at that time engaged in revival work in the California metropolis. Mr. Moody is thus quoted by Miriam Michelson, a Jewish woman, who is a very attractive special writer on that paper:

"My boy wanted a bicycle," said Mr. Moody. "He coaxed me for it. He got it. If it had been a racehorse he wanted, he should not have had it. God is truly like a father to us. He likes to be teased. Of course, his judgment is perfect, though, and in that respect my parallel to an earthly father will not hold. You think, perhaps, that if you intend to withhold something from your child, that all his coaxing will be of no avail. But you're mistaken. Ask, ask, of course."

The great revivalist sat alone upon the platform, facing the audience, at the close of yesterday's meeting. For two hours the big church had been filled to overflowing with the crowd. Yet the people filed up and past him, grasping his hand and speaking a few words to him. He was at his best just then, his short, stout body bent forward, his large, fat hand shaking cordially the many hands held up to him, his homely, kindly face in its frame of white hair falling down upon them all, even upon the six little Chinese maidens, new Christians, whom he blessed and told to "go back to China and spread the light."

"The thing to do is to pray," he said, returning to the rain question. "Why not? My little grandson has been at the point of death for nine weeks. All over the United States I have had people praying for him. He is going to recover. Why not pray for rain, then?

"Pray, I tell you! Why, I pray for everything, for anything I want, spiritual or material. I pray for everybody. I'll pray for you."

And there was an emphasis on the "you" that made it unnecessary for Mr. Moody to add the word "even."

BELIEF IN 1899.

PRESBYTERIAN VIEW.

To Rev. John Hemphill, D. D., of Calvary Presbyterian Church, is attributed the view here set forth:

Dr. Hemphill declares that it is not a miracle if rain be sent in answer to prayer.

"It is not the inversion or the change in a natural law. There is no law of Nature, or rather there is a higher law, the law of God, which sends the rain or withholds it. All this modern materialistic bathos of the scientists has nothing, absolutely, to stand upon. Tyndall probed and probed, and at the end of his researches he was honest enough to say that he could find nothing in favor of the theory of spontaneous generation. If you admit one miracle, you admit all. There are great minds that refuse to admit the miracles. There are minds as great, such as Minton's, that believe in the miracles. I believe with Minton. My faith is absolutely unshaken by such men as Huxley and Renan. I prayed for rain in my church. It was as natural a thing to do as it is for my grandchild to beg me for something he wants."

John A. B. Wilson, D. D., of Howard-Street M. E. Church, is thus quoted in answer to the inquiry: "Do you believe in prayer for rain?"

I most certainly believe in praying for rain. "Ask, and it shall be given you." In my church we prayed for rain last week. In my son's church in Pasadena they prayed for rain. There was not the sign of a cloud in the sky. There was not the slightest indication of rain. And yet rain fell, that very night.

I absolutely believe the rain fell in answer to prayer. And I am willing to go on record to that effect.

"A miracle, doctor."

"Look here, daughter," said Dr. Wilson. "Either we've got to believe in God and in the Bible, or we do not. If we do, we've got to accept God's word and his directions as given in the Bible."

Rev. William Rader, pastor of the Third Congregational Church, would not commit himself on the subject. He admitted having prayed for rain in his church, but could not be induced to be more positive than to say the necessity for miracles had passed and with it the age of miracles. Here are what I deem his most positive words:

> I am not prepared to say dogmatically that a miracle will be vouchsafed, a complete change in the laws of nature, in answer to our prayers. The miracles of Christ were, so to speak, His credentials. The necessity for miracles and their operation is a thing of the past.

Six of the most noted clergymen were interviewed and of these only two, one Jewish Rabbi, Dr. Voorsanger, and one Congregationalist, Dr. George C. Adams of the First Church, were positive in discouraging prayers for rain. Only one of those who expressed belief in the efficacy and advisability of prayer for rain would say he attributed the generous precipitation to God having pitied California farmers and granted the petitions of those who importuned him for rain.

WHY DO THEY PRAY?

A QUESTION THAT MINISTERS OF PROTESTANT CHURCHES SHOULD ANSWER.

Those who attend any orthodox church, if they pause to analyze the prayers offered therein, will wonder why they are offered. If it is true, as the average Protestant authority insists, that the age of miracles ceased with the death of the immediate successors of Peter and John, prayers are idle. Answers to prayers must come by supernatural mediums and the answers must hence be miraculous. Now if the suppliant does not believe that miracles can occur, he wastes his time when praying for the miraculous.

Do these daily, weekly or semi-weekly prayers call for miracles? If they do not, why does the Rev. Dr. Duguid beseech the Lord to bless the Sunday School of his church "in an especial manner?" This, according to my experience, is a favorite form of petition. If they do not believe in miracles, why do they pray to the Lord to endow the revivalist, who comes to re-awaken sluggish Christians and convert sinners, with especial power—inspiration for the work?

If they do not believe God will work a miracle in granting their petitions for relief to the oppressed; for the triumph of a just cause in war or politics; for wisdom and the spirit of justice to pervade the minds of legislators, executive officers and

PROTESTANT MIRACLES.

magistrates, why do they continue to repeat the petitions? I cannot resist the temptation to here comment on the strife that usually occurs before the complete organization of legislatures, and between ministers of the Gospel, for the appointment as chaplain. If, as many ministers say in private conversation, that the average legislative body is past praying for, why do they strive for the employment of offering idle, perfunctory supplications? If the average impromptu prayers of sectarian ministers do not call for miracles they mean nothing. If the printed prayers prescribed in the book of that church, so many of whose ministers like to be called priests of the holy Catholic Church, do not call for miracles they call for the exercise of great charity toward those who repeat them, much as the Thibetan grinds out a prayer from his "mill" just as their forefathers did and largely because they did.

CONCLUSION.

Lest any should consider this work incomplete because it contains no argument in favor of metaphysical healing as against the agnostics and materialists who discredit all belief in the miraculous, I simply remind readers that it was no part of my object. As a rule skeptics, "liberals," agnostics and other free thinkers have generally shown a willingness to accord to those whose teachings differ from them the same liberty they claim. If any argument is to be made against those whom the orthodox people regard as unevangelical or infidel, it must be made by others, or if made by me it must be done after I have received more light. My opinion is that, so far as mere argument goes, they are far more consistent and logical than the orthodox Christians. The only ground on which the latter argue against the credibility of present-day miracles is that of want of necessity, because the word of God is before men to read and learn for themselves. I simply wish to remind those who make the argument that the word of God was before the Pharisees and the Jews in general when Jesus was working miracles before their eyes. The Pharisees were the best educated of all the Jews and Saul of Tarsus was one of the most brilliant scholars of that sect, yet it required one of the most striking of all miracles to convert Saul, the persecutor, into Paul, the promoter, of Christianity. I would also remind them that if God is no respecter of persons He will save the poor and ignorant as well as the rich and the learned. There are millions of ignorant and poor and there are millions more of purse-proud and educated bigots whom nothing short of miracles could detach from the systems of worship and the mere mannerisms of religion. I would also remind the orthodox believer in ancient and scorner of modern miracles that, according to their belief, there is less chance of salvation for those willfully ignorant of the things celestial than for the ignorant who have had less opportunity to learn than have the wealthy, and hence that the wealthy and intelligent bigot needs miracles for his regeneration more than do the lowly.

It is no part of my purpose to argue the truth of Christian Science here. I am not authorized to speak for the church that teaches it. My argument is that self-styled orthodoxy has no warrant for assuming that the age of miracles is past; that its devotees are inconsistent in so doing while they pray for God to interpose His might to confer benefits upon them or free them from evil; that they stultify themselves when they say no miracles are performed now and in the same breath, perhaps, tell of blessings bestowed upon them or others by mysterious means. I argue that they really believe in miracles while theoretically disbelieving, just as they theoretically believe in taking no heed for the morrow, etc., but practically believe in devoting six days of the week to the acquisition of wealth and generally infringe a little on the other day, taking heed all the time for the future. I argue that they believe in miracles brought about by their own prayers and those of other members of the denominations to which they belong, but discredit those of other churches and especially those which Catholics believe in. Finally I argue that their own acts show that they believe that they disbelieve in present-day miracles, but, as was said by a droll commentator on a similar subject, "in believing that they believe they only believe they believe."

POSTSCRIPT.

Since most of the matter contained in this work was placed in the printers' hands, the anniversary of the capture of Manila by Admiral Dewey's fleet has been celebrated. At the celebrations many of the orations were delivered by clergymen of orthodox Protestant churches and in nearly all such clergymen offered invocations. In both oration and prayer the extraordinary character of the victory was, in almost every instance, attributed to the interposition of God in favor of the Americans. It is somewhat remarkable that among the clergymen so officiating and thus attributing to Dewey's victory the character of a miracle, more than one stultified himself. Among them were men who but a few months or weeks before had denounced Christian Scientists as either frauds or the dupes of a fraud because they believe that God interposes His beneficence and omniscience between man and all kinds of sin and suffering when man complies with God's laws and lives in harmony therewith.

It may be said that I have only newspaper testimony for this statement of the attitude of the clergy to miracles in this instance. That would be true, but ample time has lapsed since that celebration for those ministers who may have been incorrectly quoted to have corrected the errors, but no such corrections have come to my notice. Newspaper men of experience will accept this as the strongest endorsement that could be given of the correctness of the reports, because it has become almost a journalistic proverb that ministers always disputed reports of their utterances when their own words were quoted in refuting them or in placing them in inconsistent positions.

RECAPITULATION.

This book contains the results of several months of diligent search among the writings of eminent Protestant clergymen, authors, teachers and learned laymen who dissent from the opinion that the age of miracles had passed away long before the Reformation. It has been the object of a class to create the impression that the belief that miracles no longer occurred was general, if not universal, among Protestants of all denominations.

In this volume I have collected facts and opinions from the writings of men whose names entitle them to respect, which facts and opinions show that events which are usually classed as miracles have occurred in every century and nearly every year since the Reformation. These miracles range from inspirations for sermons to the averting of disease and danger. Although those who discredit the accounts of what appear to be miraculous healings effected by the Christian Scientists under the teachings of Mrs. Mary Baker G. Eddy, and who especially revile her claim to have had a revelation of that science, assume to do so on the strength of a pretended dogma, I find them believing in and at least impliedly teaching "special providences." I find also that men eminent in their churches have declared that they, too, were especially inspired for especial and critical occasions; that they have witnessed or experienced divine blessings in the form of rescue from death by

RECAPITULATION.

freezing, by violence of enemies, by flood, by storm; in battle and in wreck; that men have been raised up or called to the work to fill especial missions; that disease has been healed, poverty alleviated; crime prevented and criminals converted. I find among the leaders of Protestant churches many who teach or have taught in more or less crude fashion the main ideas which Mrs. Eddy has reduced to a science. I find that of those who have most bitterly attacked Mrs. Eddy's system within the range of my knowledge all, or nearly all, continue to petition God for blessings after having denounced Mrs. Eddy for doing the same thing by a different method.

I also find some very absurd discrepancies and inconsistencies in the arguments of those who attack Christian Science. Among these is the veneration in which are held some of the eminent teachers of Methodism, Baptism, Congregationalism, Presbyterianism, etc., although nearly every man thus honored taught something essentially miraculous and to that extent, in harmony with Christian Science, though they all groped in the dark as to what they called "the means of grace."

In contemplating this condition I find but one thing in Mrs. Eddy's system with which they have any logical ground for quarreling. That is what a few are brave enough to acknowledge, viz: The reduction of divine healing to a science. This has been pronounced profanation by a few. Although not openly endorsed by the many, it seems the only ground on which they can defend their action. Even this is as absurd as the action of some communities of the "Amish" Menonites who have forbidden the use of windmills by their members because they deemed it profanation to reduce God's winds to slavery by using machines that would make the elements work for man.

I find the hymnals of nearly all the churches and sects replete with evidence of either belief in miracles or poetic fictions that indicate such a belief, and I have rarely attended a religious meeting in which the prayers failed to ask for blessings, the granting of which would involve the working of miracles.

While many saintly men in the churches have been able to relieve suffering mortals, none have ever been able to teach others how to do the same work or to invest them with the power as Jesus and His apostles did. Now when Mrs. Eddy has accomplished her work, her claims to have been inspired are met by denunciation and ridicule, as presumptuous, if not blasphemous, the healings effected through her and her pupils are declared frauds, impostures or delusions, though neither she nor her students pretend that their work is miraculous. They say it is in conformity with divinely natural law and that by observing that law man may defy disease as easily as all Christians say he may defy sin.

This work is not authorized by Christian Scientists. No member of the Church of Christ has ever read a page of the manuscript or proof, nor has any of the church authorities, either local or in the headquarters in Boston, been consulted as to the expediency or propriety of publishing it.

INDEX.

Abbe, Paris	149
Afraid of the word "miracles"	170
Age of miracles	7, 139
Aid to revivalists	40, 45
Aiken's history of Presbyterianism	98
Ambrose, St.	16
Anabaptists (see Baptists)	
Anglican miracles	13
Argyll, Duke of	24
Arnold, Matthew	77
Asbury, Bishop Francis	39
Augustine, St.	11, 149
Bampton lectures	9
Baptism of the Holy Ghost	97
Baptists' testimony	64
Beecher, H. W.	11, 175
Beecher, Lyman	102
Berdoe, Dr.	135
Bernard, St.	79
Bertram's encyclopaedia	11
Blasphemer killed	120
Boehme's mysticism	136
Boss Tweed	164
Bowman, Bishop, healed	107
Boyer's history of Vaudois	20
Boy, wonder healer	123
Bruce, Professor A. M.	76
Burke, Edmund	80
Bushnell, Rev. Horace	34
Calvanist authorities	17
California miracles	121
Camp meetings, origin of	18
Carlyle, Rev. Alex	22
Cartwright, Rev. Peter	41
Catarrh cured	107
Caterpillar plague abated	48

INDEX.

Caughey, James, revivalist 56
Cave on St. Ambrose 16
Cecil, Rev. Richard 111
Charles, Mrs. E. 145
Charlatan cures, etc. 93
Christian age 117
Christlieb, Professor Theo. 87
Christian Science 77, 85
Clarke, Dr. E. H. 90
Cobbe, Francis Power 159
College professors' views 71
Communing with God 59
Combinations of forces 103
Congregation converted 54
Conversion like Paul's 96
Conclusion 185
Cranmer on divine selections 13
Credulity and incredulity 33
Cumberland Presbyterians 18
Curtis, Rev. Lucius 151
Cyclone diverted 50
Dabney, Professor R. L. 140

Davy, Sir Humphrey 162
Dead raised 40
Debt miraculously paid 177
Deceit attributed to Jesus 78
Degrees in miracles 153
Deserting husbands converted 107, 114
Dictation to Omnipotence 143
Disbelief and results 7
Dyspepsia healed 107
Divine guidance 18, 39, 48, 60, 99
Divine wrath 164
Doubt of God's power 98
Drunkard converted 53
Duke of Argyll 24
Duke of Savoy 22
Dwight, Professor Timothy 81

Ears do not hear 92
Eddy, Mrs. Mary B. 130

INDEX.

Edwards, "Sailor"	69
Egede, Hans	89
Elizabeth, Queen	13
Episcopal church	13
Escape from disease	46
Evans'. history of Shakers	140
Evangelists' miracles	38
Evidence of miracles	137
Eyes do not see	92
Farrar, Canon	15, 119
Fasting for miracles	30, 54
Fed miraculously	69
Ferrier, Dr. David	92
Ferriage provided for	142
Finney, Professor C. G.	18, 95
Fisher, Professor George P.	79
Fiske, Professor John	86
Fog in aid of Vaudois	21
Fowler, Bishop C. H.	49
Fox, George	152
French fleet destroyed	81
Gairdner, James	142
George, Bishop, healed	53
Giles, Rev. Chauncy	45
Gilly, William Stephen	16, 21
God raises up men	18
God guided Puritans	29
God defeats a trickster	31
God swept the strings	133
Godet, F.	74
Greatrakes, Valentine	157
Gregory, St.	11, 148
Gruber, Rev. Jacob	45
Harris, Professor Samuel	80
Harvard college	17
Hatfield, Dr. E. F.	108
Hays' Presbyterian history	17
Healing by prayer	44, 53, 65, 107, 116
Healing by royal touch	85

INDEX.

Hemphill, Rev. John 181
Henry VIII 14
Hensoldt, Dr. Heinrich 141
Hohensbell, the healer 124
Holmes, Oliver Wendell 90
Holbrook, Rev. J. C. 174
Holy coat of Treves 16
Hopkins, Professor Mark 103
Hospital walls prayed up 118
Howitt, William 11
Humboldt 162
Hume 144, 163
Huxley 10, 152, 163
Hymns for miracles 128

Illustration by miracle 112
Indian mortality aids Puritans 32
Infidel testimony 152
Inskip, William 108
Inspiration of preachers 18, 48, 99, 117
Inspiration for paying cash 117
Inspiration in general 138

Jansenist miracles 149, 163
Jerks (religious contortions) 38, 42
Jesting to deny fact 36
Jones, Bishop 107
Jones, Rev. Sam 47
Judd, Carrie F. 109
Judgment on sinners 43

Keach, Benjamin 67
Kiffen, Rev. William 68
Killed by imagination 124
Kinnear, J. Boyd, on cure 143
Knapp, Elder Jacob 40
Knollys, Rev. Hanserd 65
Kostlin, Julius 74
Krummacher, Rev. Dr. 118, 177

Labor divinely rewarded 100
Lama, Grand, of Thibet 141

INDEX.

Law, "Reign of" 24
Law above human ken 25
Law of nature 27, 75
Law, higher 77
Law, combination of 50
Law, William 136
Lee, Mother Ann 140
Lecky on doubt 10, 152
Liefchild, Dr. 119
Life miraculously saved 50
Life without brain 92
Limiting Omnipotence 145, 158
Liquified air 126
Locke, on natural law 27
Luther's belief 74, 116, 120
Lutheran witness 150

Macaulay on Cranmer 13
McAdow's revelation 18
McLeod, Rev. Donald 111
Maffitt, J. Newland 44
Mahaffy, J. P. 27
Mallock on Huxley 10
Manfred, Jacob 155
Marpingen miracles 152
Marion, General Frances 155
Marriage prevented 59
Mark of Arethusa 165
Marsden, Rev. Joshua 39
Mather, Cotton and Increase 32
Methodists and miracles 38
Melancthon healed 89, 116
Menno, Simon 64
Mennonites (see Baptists) ....
Middleton, Conyers, on disbelief 15
Millman's history 164
Minister converted 57
Miracles, of healing 44, 53, 65, 107, 116
Miracles, for illustration 112
Miracles, defined 8, 169
Miracles, Baptists 10
Miracles, Methodists .... 38 to 61, 69

INDEX.

Miracles, miscellaneous .... 135 to 146
Miracles and Providences 10
Miracles, Tractarian 154
Miracles, non-religious 121
Miracles, workers expelled 14
Miracles, in 1899 179
Moody, Dwight L. 110, 179
Moravian example 145
Mormon miracle 167
Mysterious circulation of news 126
Mysticism—Boehme's 136
Neumark, George 132
Newman, Cardinal 12, 129
Newspaper miracles 126
News mysteriously circulated 126
New Ulm massacre 164

Oberlin college 100

Paris, Abbe 149
Popular Science Monthly 152
Porter, Professor Noah 81
Prayer, Efficacy of 45, 49, 57, 67
Prayer, Power of 67, 81, 103, 110 118
Prayer, Gauge 140
Prayer, For temporal concerns 118
Prayer, Cure (orthodox) 56
Precocious prophet 22
Presbyterians quoted .... 17 to 27
Postscript 187
Princes divinely appointed 13
Protestant repression 14
Providences and miracles 10
Providence guides an arrow 20
Providential immigration 19
Puritan miracles .... 28 to 33

Quaker marvels 34, 152

Rader, Rev. William 182
Rain by prayer 30, 103
Recapitulation 188

INDEX.

Reformation a miracle 17, 21
Relics and miracles 15, 153
Rescue from robbers 111
Rescue from starvation 111
Rescue from pirates 112
Results of disbelief 7, 35
Revelations to men 18, 34, 41, 60, 64
Robinson, Rev. Frederick 177
Rockyzan, John 145
Russian miracle workers 86,

San Francisco clergymen 179
Saved for the church 51
Saved from starvation 30, 130
Saved from wreck 29, 32, 89
Scientists rebuke skeptics 162
Scoffer converted 52
Scoffer killed 43
Scotch believers 22
Schu, Karl Gottlob 106
Schwenkfeldians 14
Simpson, Bishop, healed 107
Shaker marvels 140
Skeptic credulity 141, 148, 153
Slander refuted 34
Smith, Jennie 109
Smith, Rev. John 142
Soldier's life saved 119
Specious orthodox reasoning 139
Spirit perceived 94
Spurgeon's views 70, 89, 114
Stephens, Sir James 153
Steffens, Heinrich 150
Sunday school miracles 16

Talmage, Rev. T. D. 164
Taylor, Bishop William 107
Tractarian miracles 154
Traitor stricken dumb 65
Trench, Archbishop 169
Tyndall's views 10, 140

INDEX.

Union Theological Seminary 74, 77
Unseen world 86
Unwelcome preacher 53
Usher, Archbishop 113

Vaudois 20
Visions, marvelous 90
Vision of Professor Finney 97

War miracles 80
Warburton, Bishop 144
Ware, Dr., of Boston 93
Wace, Bishop, on Huxley 10
Waldenses (see Vaudois)
Wallace, Alfred R. 162
Watson, Dr. James V. 52
Wesley 39, 119
Weather affected by prayer 49
Wilson, Rev. J. A. B. 181
Witchcraft 32
Wonders of science 25
Williams, Roger 70
White, Andrew D. 83
White discredits himself 84
Why do they pray 183
Why they are incensed 172
Wreck averted 89

Yale professors' views 79

www.ingramcontent.com/pod-product-compliance
Lightning Source LLC
Chambersburg PA
CBHW021734220426
43662CB00008B/839